LOUISIANA'S
OLD STATE CAPITOL

LOUISIANA'S
OLD STATE CAPITOL

CAROL K. HAASE

PELICAN PUBLISHING COMPANY
GRETNA 2009

Library of Congress Cataloging-in-Publication Data

Haase, Carol K.
Louisiana's old State Capitol / by Carol K. Haase.
p. cm.
Includes bibliographical references and index.
ISBN 978-1-58980-615-3 (pbk. : alk. paper) 1. Louisiana State Capitol (Baton Rouge, La.)—History. 2. Historic buildings—Conservation and restoration—Louisiana—Baton Rouge. 3. Public buildings—Conservation and restoration—Louisiana—Baton Rouge. 4. Baton Rouge (La.)—Buildings, structures, etc. 5. Baton Rouge (La.)—History. I. Title.
F379.B33H23 2009
976.3'18—dc22

2008042022

Printed in the United States of America

Published by Pelican Publishing Company, Inc.
1000 Burmaster Street, Gretna, Louisiana 70053

Contents

Chapter One: Baton Rouge Becomes Capital 9
Chapter Two: Building in Baton Rouge 13
Chapter Three: The Early Years 19
Chapter Four: Civil War and Reconstruction 29
Chapter Five: Returning to Baton Rouge 35
Chapter Six: Rebuilding the Castle 39
Chapter Seven: Good Times and Bad 49
Chapter Eight: Peace to Pandemonium 57
Chapter Nine: Abandonment 67
Chapter Ten: Fight for Identity and Resurrection 75
Appendix I: Cast Iron Lace—The Surrounding Fence 93
Appendix II: Henry Watkins Allen Monument 99
Appendix III: Inaugurations of Governors
Who Served in the State House 105
Appendix IV: The Merci Train 111
Notes 115
Bibliography 132
Index 133

LOUISIANA'S
OLD STATE CAPITOL

Chapter One

Baton Rouge Becomes Capital

In a most unlikely place, a modest Southern town near the Gulf of Mexico, a Gothic castle calmly reigns over the meanderings of the Mississippi River. The unusual structure, completed in 1850, was built in Baton Rouge as the State House of Louisiana. The dignified exterior of the building gives no hint of the colorful and sometimes explosive Louisiana politics played out within its walls. But the road to Baton Rouge began far away almost one hundred and fifty years earlier.

Before the Louisiana Purchase in 1803, French explorers sailed down the Mississippi River and claimed for France the river and all the territory drained by it. The ill-defined, unexplored area was passed between France and Spain as political strategy and monetary matters dictated. The goal of those two loosely allied countries was to keep the territory out of British hands, even at the ultimate cost of selling it to the new nation, the United States.

New Orleans was colonized by the French in 1718 and became the largest city in the territory. Its location between the Mississippi River and Lake Pontchartrain allowed France to protect its territory by controlling the mouth of the river. Other locations on higher ground were certainly better suited for a habitable colony, but the strategic location overrode the need for comfort. The colonized land was generally marshy and below sea level. Conditions were harsh. Mosquitoes, reptiles, heat, and humidity made living conditions less than ideal; yet in spite of all the negatives, the colony grew, and later, under Spanish rule, it even flourished. But New Orleans, as well as the entire Louisiana territory, was not a profitable venture for either France or Spain and proved to be a financial drain on those countries in constant need of funds for their war chests.

Threatened with shipping and trade problems at the mouth of the river, Pres. Thomas Jefferson authorized Robert Livingston, American minister to France, and James Monroe, a former minister to France (1794-1796), to negotiate for the purchase of the Isle of Orleans, the area around New Orleans and the mouth of the river.[1] French emperor Napoleon Bonaparte presented them with an offer too incredible to refuse. For approximately fifteen million dollars in cash and assumption of debt, the United States agreed to purchase over 800,000 square miles, giving the United States absolute control over the entire Mississippi River. After the territory became part of the United States, Americans rushed to New Orleans, making it a wonderful mixture of nationalities and races.

In 1812, Louisiana became the first state admitted from the Louisiana Territory, and the seat of government was established at New Orleans. It was not long, however, before legislators were pressured to remove themselves from the big city and its attractions. Rural planters elected to the legislature were reportedly spending their days taking care of their own personal business—selling and shipping crops. At night, they were taking advantage of the pleasures of the city, which, even today, make New Orleans a world-famous tourist destination. The performance of elected civil servants fell short of the electorate's expectations, and a movement to get the legislators away from the city's temptations was born.[2]

In 1825, the legislature voted to move the state capital to Donaldsonville. A commission was appointed to prepare and furnish legislative chambers, and provisions were made to move the state archives.[3] A capitol building was erected in Donaldsonville, and the legislature held its first session away from New Orleans in 1830. The legislators of 1831 convened in the new capital, but, missing the amenities of the big city, they immediately voted to return the seat of government to New Orleans.[4] After only one year and one week in Donaldsonville, the legislature returned to the former capital city.

The legislature of 1843 moved the seat of government from New Orleans to Baton Rouge.[5] The vote received almost no journalistic notice, and the move was never made. It is possible the legislature anticipated a constitutional convention and saw no need to move until the matter was settled by a vote of the people.

In 1845, a new constitution was proposed which required the legislature to

> designate and fix the seat of government at some place not less than sixty miles from the city of New Orleans by the nearest traveling route, and if on the Mississippi River, by the meanders of the same, and, when so fixed, it shall not be removed without the consent of four-fifths of the members of both houses of the general assembly.[6]

A four-fifths majority was an almost insurmountable obstacle and meant the capital would not return to New Orleans without overwhelming support for such a move. In the 1840s, sixty miles was approximately a fifteen-hour trip[7], more than one could expect to travel in a day. Legislators would be unable to get to New Orleans for an evening of dinner and theater, then return (or fail to return) to the capital for the next day's business. They could not be wined, dined, and influenced by lobbyists and pressure groups, but would be forced to take care of business for lack of anything more entertaining to do. A Baton Rouge newspaper, the *Democratic Advocate,* reported that it felt the new constitution would be overwhelmingly approved "to the utter dismay and confusion of all aristocrats."[8] The constitution was approved, and in 1846, the legislature named Baton Rouge the capital city of Louisiana.[9]

Chapter Two

Building in Baton Rouge

Perhaps to sweeten the deal and to ensure the town would be chosen, Baton Rouge offered to donate a suitable site for the State House in exchange for being named state capital. It was not a large town, but its proud citizens pooled their resources to bid for the honor.[1]

The legislature, still meeting in New Orleans, began planning for the State House. Maunsel White, George Cook, and Walter Brashear were named commissioners to supervise construction.[2] At that time, all three men were either current or former legislators. In January of 1847, newspapers published advertisements calling for submissions of architectural plans for a State House. Just three days later, James Harrison Dakin submitted his design.

James Dakin was born in New York, where he established a reputation as an outstanding architect. In 1835, he followed his brother Charles to New Orleans and built a successful career designing buildings throughout the South.[3]

In a letter to the commissioners, Dakin stated three goals. The first was to provide adequate rooms and offices for conducting state business. He anticipated that forty-two rooms would be sufficient for the present and foreseeable future. Second, he wanted to give the building "a decided distinctive, classic, and commanding character." Dakin believed that a design of the popular Greek or Roman style would have no distinction but would only copy buildings and state houses found in other large cities and capitals. He preferred what he considered a unique "Castellated Gothic" style. His third aim was to provide these things in the most economical manner. He estimated a cost of $100,000 if the building were made of brick and $200,000 if made of marble.[4]

With the letter, Dakin submitted his architectural plan, a "plain geometric drawing." He explained that the simple sketch of the building should stand on its own merits without attempts to distract the commissioners through lavish landscaping and coloring. He added that he was certain they were intelligent and tasteful enough to see through any effort to fool them by adding unnecessary embellishments. The commissioners wrote Dakin asking for more detailed information about building materials and cost estimates.[5]

It is not known how many architectural plans were submitted; however, the commissioners must have been impressed with Dakin's design, because they did not wait for the end of the three-month bid period before presenting their selection to the legislature. Other architects were outraged by the premature adoption of Dakin's plan and wrote to the commission expressing their fury.[6] They were unsuccessful in their attempt to have their designs considered, and on May 4, 1847, Dakin received official notice that his design for the State House had been selected. The letter was signed by White and Brashear, a majority of the commissioners. The third commissioner, Cook, resigned rather than accept Dakin's design. There were many reasons for Cook's refusal of the design, among them the hastiness of the selection. Even so, Dakin harshly criticized him, saying Cook was not interested in the state's economy but in his personal gain as a commissioner.[7] Daniel Avery, who served as state representative from 1832 to 1836, was appointed to replace Cook. Dakin's letters and those of the commissioners were all recorded in a diary kept by the architect. During the selection process, and throughout construction, he meticulously recorded all aspects of contracts, orders, costs, and labor, as well as numerous problems. Fortunately, the diary survived and is now in the Louisiana and Lower Mississippi Valley Collections, LSU Libraries, Baton Rouge, Louisiana.

While the commissioners searched for an architect, Baton Rouge searched for the perfect site for the new State House. The town council and police jury each appropriated five thousand dollars toward the purchase of a site. The first site selected was rejected because there were problems with the title.[8] Local newspapers called for property owners to "come forward, be reasonable in their demands, and to do all in their power to effect the great object in view."[9]

The property of Judge Thomas Gibbs Morgan was finally chosen. Described as one of the most beautiful and impressive sites on the river,[10] it was bordered on the north by North Boulevard, on the east by St. Philip Street, on the south by America Street, and on the west by Natchez Street (River Road). The land, approximately five acres and valued at twenty thousand dollars, was officially transferred to the state on September 22, 1847, for the sole purpose of constructing a building for use by the legislature and elected officials.[11]

Before any final plans were made, the legislature added fifty thousand dollars to the original construction estimate of $100,000 to provide higher-quality building materials and to pay the architect. The commissioners engaged a local firm, McHatton, Pratt & Co., to provide bricks and timber. A Pittsburgh company, Knapp & Totten, received the contract to provide structural and decorative iron.[12]

As early as July of 1847, well before the official land transfer, workmen had cleared the property and were hauling materials to the construction site. Because the actual placing of bricks could not begin until October, Dakin arranged a trip to Pittsburgh to work on designs for the iron to be used in construction. En route, his plans were stolen. His young son witnessed the theft, and the drawings were retrieved. [13]

Dakin returned to Baton Rouge in October to begin construction. The site chosen was some of the first high ground on the Mississippi River. Fixing the exact location of the State House on the land was a primary concern. According to Dakin, the commissioners chose the placement on the northeast corner of the site, twenty-five feet from St. Philip Street and seventy-five feet from North Boulevard, to avoid the low, irregular edge of the property closest to the river. Even though low parts of Baton Rouge and the surrounding area had occasionally flooded, the high corner on which the State House was being built had not been under water. Ground was broken on October 26, 1847.[14]

Excitement ran high in Baton Rouge as the dream of being state capital became tangible. Plans were made to lay the cornerstone on November 3. That day, a crowd anxious to take part in the festivities gathered on the State House grounds. Members of the local St. James Lodge, Free and Accepted Masons invited the Grand Lodge of Louisiana from New Orleans to help conduct the 10:00 A.M. ceremony. The New Orleans group had arranged to travel by steamer, but no steamer arrived at the appointed time. Finally, about mid-afternoon, the tardy guests, accompanied by a band, arrived at the dock. The ceremony called for numerous speeches, but one eloquent orator outdid himself by delivering a two-hour address in French. Because it was getting dark, other scheduled speeches were eliminated with the exception of an abbreviated address by commissioner Daniel Avery, who thanked Baton Rouge for procuring such an impressive site. A collection was taken to aid the poor.

Following the ceremony, lodge members indulged in a joyful feast. At 9:00 P.M., after "many excellent and patriotic toasts," the group formed a procession and marched through the streets of town, each person holding a lighted candle. The next morning members of the Grand Lodge departed aboard the same steamer that had brought them. All had enjoyed the jubilant celebration, which was fitting for a building of such status.[15] Researchers have been unable to determine just where the cornerstone was laid. Years later, it was revealed in an unrelated article that a copy of the magazine *Magnolia*, a note to posterity, and some silver coins were among the items placed in it. The coins proved too great a lure to a thief who broke open the cornerstone and made away with the contents.[16]

Once the celebration was over, the real work of constructing the State House began. In December, the first shipment of iron arrived, and a load of bricks was delivered. Dakin considered the bricks to be of inferior quality and stopped work until they could be replaced. Dakin made his first written report to the commissioners in January of 1848. By then, the foundation was complete, and approximately ten feet of the basement walls had been built.

At first, construction went smoothly, but later, lack of building materials caused incessant delays. Brickwork could not proceed because iron was needed. When the iron arrived, more bricks were needed, and so forth throughout the entire building process.[17]

Delays were not the only problem. Dakin was also plagued by deliveries of building materials of inferior quality. He refused several shipments of iron. In May of 1848, Dakin became furious with Knapp & Totten and accused them of trying to dispose of their iron by padding the thickness. He assured them that no matter what the thickness of the delivered iron, the state would pay only at the rate of the requested thickness. Ever the frugal watchman, he later criticized them for weighing the iron after packing it in the shipping boxes. He had everything reweighed, deducted the weight of the shipping boxes, and paid only for the iron.[18]

Frequently, loads of soft and crumbly inferior bricks were delivered to the building site. Dakin's frustration finally reached the boiling point in August 1848. While workmen were installing the soft bricks in the walls, the angry architect threw the bricks off the scaffolding, tore them out of the walls, and tossed them to the ground. The contractor, William Pratt, approached Dakin, and a fight broke out. Although neither man was injured, the mayor had them both arrested for disorderly conduct and fined three dollars. Dakin was fined an additional ten dollars because he had thrown the first punch.[19] The bad-brick argument continued throughout construction. Mr. McHatton, one of the company owners, returned to town after an extended absence and assured everyone concerned that the contract for high-quality, hard bricks would be honored.[20] That solved the immediate problem, but peace did not last for long. As little as one week later, work stopped again for want of quality bricks.

In spite of delays and lack of materials throughout 1849, construction progressed slowly. By August, the roof was in place over both legislative chambers. In September, plasterwork began on the interior.

Construction wound down, and workmen began to leave in January of 1850, just as the legislature planned to meet for the first time in its new home. On January 10, the last entry in Dakin's diary shows that he received final payment for his work. The total cost of the building, just under $400,000, almost quadrupled Dakin's original estimate.[21]

The people of Baton Rouge anticipated a glorious dedication ceremony and grand opening of the State House, but it was not to be. In late November of 1849, mere weeks before the legislature was to meet, a disastrous fire destroyed much of Baton Rouge. Believed to be the work of arsonists intent on looting, the fire leveled entire blocks of downtown Baton Rouge. The area destroyed was bordered by Lafayette Street, Church (Fourth) Street, North Street, and Water Street.[22] The mood of the town was not one of celebration. Money earmarked for a grand dedication ceremony was diverted to aid the victims of the ruinous fire.[23]

Chapter Three

The Early Years

Louisiana government slowly settled into the new State House during the 1850s. When the legislature met for the first time in Baton Rouge, construction on the capitol building was not yet finished. At the end of January in 1850, Gov. Isaac Johnson addressed the legislature and expressed regret that legitimate delays had prevented contractors from completing the State House.[1] Although incomplete, the building was far enough along for the legislature to convene and for the citizens of Baton Rouge to enjoy its use.

One minor item brought before the legislature of 1850 received little more than a brief mention in the *Baton Rouge Gazette,* but it was to have serious consequences in the years to come. The legislative committee on contingent expenses considered obtaining special fire equipment, an engine, and a fire hose for the State House. Dakin was consulted. He told the committee that the State House was designed in such a way that there was little danger of its catching fire; therefore, he believed it unnecessary to purchase extra fire safety equipment for the State House. The committee agreed, and the matter was dropped.[2]

Construction continued for many months after the building opened. The legislature of 1852 appropriated $26,500 to complete the State House.[3] Just as the finishing touches were nearing completion, James Dakin died in Baton Rouge. A simple obituary appeared in the *Baton Rouge Gazette.* "DIED, In this parish, at his residence, after a long and painful illness, on Thursday evening, the 19th, inst. Col. James H. Dakin."[4] There is speculation about where he is buried, but the site of his grave remains unknown, as well as the cause of his death.

The 1850s in Louisiana were distinguished by two things. Foremost was the constant bickering between Baton Rouge and

New Orleans. Both cities engaged in vicious rhetoric over the question of which one should rightfully be capital. The other was the effort to maintain and modernize the State House and its beautiful grounds.

If Baton Rouge expected jubilation from the rest of the state for being designated the new capital, it was mistaken. As early as 1848, while construction of the State House was still in progress, the citizens of New Orleans began to understand the reality of their impending loss. The people of the city were determined not to lose their prized distinction without a fight. The legislature of that year entertained a motion to keep the capital in New Orleans. It was tabled, but that failed motion was noteworthy because it was the first shot fired in a battle that would continue for almost one hundred years.[5]

The New Orleans press, downright indignant that the capital had been removed from its city, asked, "Is it possible the state of Louisiana *can really exist out of the limits of New Orleans?*"[6] The *New Orleans Bee,* a French- and English-language newspaper, declared that both the governor and the governor-elect had become ill due to the lack of conveniences in Baton Rouge and it would only be a short time before the capital returned to New Orleans.[7] A French-language publication said legislators would realize the inconvenience of being in Baton Rouge the minute personal business interests required their presence in New Orleans. According to *Le Courrier de la Louisiane,* legislators would be entirely deprived of documents and the information necessary to make good laws. The enactment of bad laws would quickly force them away from Baton Rouge if sheer boredom did not do it first.[8]

The barrage of insults did not stop even after the building was occupied by state officials. A New Orleans publication, the *Bulletin,* said that being in Baton Rouge had placed the legislature "beyond the reach of LIGHT, KNOWLEDGE!! and VIRTUE!!! . . . It is too far removed from the centre of intelligence, and the immediate influence of a daily and vigilant press." Another New Orleans publication, the *Delta,* was quoted as calling the new State House a "Semi-Barbaric Castle of 'olden times,'" and described it as an uncomfortable, "mis-shapen mass of bricks" that had cost the people over $300,000.[9] With newly found bravado, the *Baton Rouge Gazette* responded by stating that moving the capital "has placed our legislature beyond the influence of rich corporations, fine dinners, excelling wines, and other stimulants, through which in times gone by, certain moneyed individuals used to have pretty much their own way, in the legislation of the State."[10]

In 1850, as the first legislature was meeting, the *Southern Sentinel* of Plaquemine, Louisiana, reported that because legislators were dissatisfied with Baton Rouge, and often visited "the city," little was being accomplished in the legislature. The reporter predicted that the capital would return to New Orleans and construction of the State House would never be completed.[11] A similar complaint was logged in 1854 by the *Natchitoches Chronicle,* which asserted that a minimum of two days per week were wasted due to a lack of quorums.[12]

The former capital, in an effort to regain its position, presented an all-out assault on Baton Rouge in 1853. Baton Rouge was accused of lacking accommodations and amenities. The Board of Aldermen of the City of New Orleans passed a resolution offering to donate Congo Square if the capital were moved back.[13] Congo Square (in the area now known as Louis Armstrong Park, near the Municipal Auditorium) was a large field where slaves and free blacks gathered on Sundays to socialize, dance, and sell produce and handmade items. The Mechanic's Institute building (site of the capitol from 1866 to 1874), the Odd Fellows Hall, and Charity Hospital were also offered as possible legislative quarters.[14] An unnamed representative suggested soliciting the estate of deceased New Orleans philanthropist Judah Touro to fund the building of a capitol on Canal Street as a monument to the donor and using the present State House as a school named Touro University.[15]

An anonymous article in the *New Orleans Christian Advocate* had perhaps the unkindest cut of all. It compared Baton Rouge to moss and mistletoe on the oak tree, a parasite that enjoyed the bounty of the tree but had no visible means of support.[16] It was a rare legislative session when no bill was introduced to return the capital to New Orleans. In 1855, a resolution to move the capital narrowly passed the Senate, but advanced no further.[17] Finally, in 1860, the Baton Rouge press had heard enough and reported that it would willingly relinquish the seat of government if the New Orleans press would stop abusing and slandering Baton Rouge and stop insulting the remainder of the state by implying that it was fit for nothing but pasture and farmland to supply the big city.[18]

Even though the State House was still fairly new, it received constant use and needed periodic upkeep and repair. Legislators treated it less than reverently. The *Weekly Comet* likened them to "cur dogs" for spitting tobacco juice in the corners, leaving wads of tobacco and cigar ends on the rugs, whittling and leaving scattered wood shavings, and propping their legs on the mahogany desks.[19] With several references to wine and whiskey in historic records, it is easy to believe early legislative sessions were animated, if not downright rowdy. The *Weekly Comet* of 1853 said the wine reservoir on top of one of the western towers was almost ready.[20] In January of 1854, a spell of unusually hot weather caused tanks at the capitol to be filled with cool water instead of the previously arranged "hot whiskey punch" although an "anti-spasmodic elixer" was provided at state expense under the budget heading "candle account."[21] When legislative sessions ended, everything was left either where it was or so damaged as to be unusable for another session. Legislators were apparently not above a bit of white-collar crime—the *Weekly Comet* accused them of pilfering stationary and other small items at the close of legislative sessions."[22]

Certainly, most repairs were not necessitated by human mistreatment. The State House was plagued with an architectural design problem, which caused the roof to leak during Louisiana's frequent rains. Gutters on the roof were supposed to carry rainwater to drain pipes embedded in the walls. Although the design was aesthetically pleasing because no gutters hung down the outside walls, the pipes were inadequate to hold large amounts of water and often became clogged during heavy rains.

In 1852, the legislature appropriated $2,500 for repairs. Two years later, more repairs were necessary. By 1856, leakage was so bad that not only the building, but also the State Library, the archives, and everything else were in danger of being soaked. The library, located on the third floor, had "scarcely a space ten feet square" where anything was safe from the destructive water.[23] A local newspaper, the *Weekly Morning Comet,* prepared to launch a private subscription drive (proposed by Baton Rougeans proud of the State House) to raise money for the repairs,[24] but by the end of 1856, the much-needed repairs were under way.

Another design problem, which caused understandable complaint, was lack of water for "ablution purposes." A local entrepreneur built a facility, probably a barbershop, on Lafayette Street with the hope of attracting legislators to wash and shave; water was pumped into the building from the river by steam engine.[25] Legislators also complained about the darkness of the rooms in the State House. The building was designed to let in an abundance of natural light, but the center of the building, the rotunda, and the hallways were almost always dark. A small six-by-nine-foot skylight in the roof was woefully inadequate to light the interior of the building.[26] Therefore, in 1857, the legislature appropriated funds to light the State House with gas, provided it did not cost more that $3,500.[27] Workers dug two large reservoirs holding about 3500 cubic feet of gas in the basement and cut through floors, brick walls, and ceilings to extend the necessary pipes to each room.[28] By January of 1858, gas lights illuminated the capitol. Townspeople loved it and thought the building had "a halo about as bright as day," and since gas was cheaper than candles, great savings were expected. The only possible downside to the new gas apparatus was explained, "Now there will be no further cost and no room for smuggling wines, liquors, segars, etc., into the building under the head of 'candles.'"[29]

Throughout the decade, the legislature proposed ambitious projects solely to beautify and embellish the State House and grounds. One of the largest undertakings involved commissioning a patriotic statue. The first floor of the State House contained a large rotunda in which the commissioners and the architect intended to place a statue of George Washington. The legislature of 1850 contracted with Hiram Powers, an American sculptor living in Florence, Italy, to create the statue of marble. In 1853, the *Weekly Comet* questioned the whereabouts of the anticipated sculpture.[30] When Powers responded that the 6-foot, 7½-inch figure would soon be finished, questions arose regarding safe placement of and proper lighting for the sculpture. The rotunda was dark and the plank floor was inadequate to hold the large statue securely, but nothing was done to address the problems.

When the long-awaited statue finally arrived in Baton Rouge in June of 1855, the State House was not structurally ready to receive it. The inexcusable procrastination was severely criticized by the press, who thought no amount of apology would be sufficient to atone for such negligence.[31] It took almost three years before alterations began, which would allow the "Father of Our Country" to be properly displayed. The small skylight above the rotunda was enlarged to equal the size of the second- and third-floor openings, allowing more natural light in the center of the building.[32] The next January, workmen prepared a foundation for the heavy statue.[33] Four years passed after George Washington's arrival before it was set in its intended location. During those years, it was housed on the northwest side of the building in an elaborate but much maligned "pagoda," or "coop," which cost the state fifteen thousand dollars.[34] By the summer of 1859, nine years after its commissioning, the statue of George Washington was in place and popular with the viewing public.[35] Unfortunately, George Washington's stay at the Louisiana State House would be brief.

A long-feared catastrophe occurred on March 31, 1856. A flagstaff on the northwest tower burned and fell to the ground, alerting people below to a fire. Firefighters responded quickly and found flames on the tower roof. A leather fire hose was brought up the stairs and through the House chamber. The pressure of pumping water to such a great height caused the hose to burst in several places, flooding the House chamber. As reported by the *Weekly Morning Comet,* some bystanders thought quickly enough to pull curtains from the House chamber windows and wrap them around the split hoses. Others, afraid the engines and hoses would fail, formed a bucket brigade up the steps and to the tower. "Daring firemen" and ordinary citizens were "tearing up the burning materials with their hands and throwing them over the battlements, flaming with the devouring element."[36] Vandals were suspected of starting the Sunday evening fire, which destroyed the roof of the northwest tower and caused extensive water damage to the House chamber. It was the custom to leave the capitol open but unattended on Sundays to allow visitors access to the building. Even though the damage was extensive, the State House was mercifully spared from complete destruction.

Legislators and vandals were not the only people frequenting the State House. The citizens of Baton Rouge had found a beautiful, convenient venue for programs, concerts, and parties. In 1850, on the anniversary of Washington's birthday, a gala ball was held in the rotunda. Tickets sold for two dollars apiece. The *Baton Rouge Gazette* reported that flags were hanging from every corner of the room. Military paraphernalia—muskets and artillery—were on display. Members of the Washington Guard Company dressed in full military finery, and civilians wore "serious" dress. The ladies, with their bright eyes and bewitching smiles, were exceptionally lovely. The ball was by far the most lavish event that had ever been held in Baton Rouge.[37] In 1854, the walls of the House chamber reverberated with the sounds of three famous musicians in concert: Ole Bull, Maurice Strakosch, and Adelina Patti.[38] Another gala event, the Grand Fancy Dress Anniversary Ball, which included dancing to a band from "the city," was held on the anniversary of Washington's birthday in 1855. Tickets were sold at the then-substantial sum of five dollars. The editors of the *Weekly Comet* reported a dilemma, as the ball occurred on the second day of Lent, when fasting and abstinence were required. Their simple solution was to seek an indulgence beforehand or absolution afterward.[39] In 1856, an estimated audience of four hundred people, including Gov. Robert Charles Wickliffe, attended a concert of opera selections presented by a troupe traveling the river.[40] In one month of 1858 alone, both the Presbyterian and Methodist ladies held grand entertainments in the State House, and a visiting musician performed a violin concert in the House of Representatives.[41] At the end of the 1858 session, the legislature held a farewell ball that lasted until the wee hours of the morning.[42] The State House was even rented out for commercial ventures. In 1857, opticians opened an office on the third floor across from, appropriately enough, the State Library.[43]

The grounds surrounding the State House were a great source of pride, but by 1854, they were in need of beautification and upkeep. The legislature provided funds to improve the grounds by planting trees and shrubs and otherwise beautifying the area—a total sum of $21,630.24 was allotted for beautification.[44] They called for walkways leading to the capitol and an eight-foot wide brick banquette (sidewalk) around the square. An iron fence surrounding the entire grounds proved to be the most enduring of the improvements. The legislature was very specific in its description of the fence, requesting a height of five to seven feet and ironwork set in a granite foundation. The picket fence that originally surrounded the square was removed and donated to the Female Orphan Association of Baton Rouge. By October, the contract for the new fence had been let, but work had not begun. Locals feared that if it were not built soon, the legislature would find some other use for the appropriated funds at the next session.[45] Fortunately, by January of 1855, construction of the iron fence was well under way. The *Weekly Comet* described it in this manner: "The pattern is not only beautiful in design, but combines the strength necessary for the work. The fence is supported by iron bolts worked into the brick work, and a cap, or rather base, of cast iron covers, the wall projecting four inches on either side."[46]

In 1859, lamps were added to the main (west) entrance,[47] and landscaping was completed.

> The work of terracing is done, and all the trees, shrubs and flowers, are growing finely. The walks have been protected with shells, and the place has the appearance of a flower garden. The neatness and order of the grounds attract the ladies and children there in the evening, and it is getting to be a fashionable place to resort.[48]

This was the first mention that the hill sloping from the State House to the Mississippi River had been terraced.

In spite of the many problems, everything had come together to make a beautiful State House, one the people of Louisiana could regard with pride. In grandiose fashion, the *Weekly Gazette & Comet* boasted, "We are proud of it, because there is nothing like it on the continents—because it is planted firmly, in the eternal hill, to look on the mighty Mississippi to the very running down of sublunar time."[49] Little did anyone realize that time was short, and very dark days were on the horizon.

Chapter Four

Civil War and Reconstruction

By the 1860s, Louisiana, as well as the entire country, was consumed with the debates over slavery, states' rights, and secession. Reflecting the serious times, the legislature of 1860 passed a resolution forbidding use of the State House for anything but legislative and political gatherings.[1] Formerly a hub of social and political activity, the State House suddenly became the stage where acts of tremendous historical consequence were played out. In December of 1860, Gov. Thomas Overton Moore called for a special legislative session to discuss the state's position on secession, but writers for the *Gazette & Comet* sensed that the matter had already been quietly agreed upon by the delegates.[2] On Saturday, January 26, 1861, with only seventeen dissenting votes, the legislature voted to remove Louisiana from the United States of America. The scene was described in the *Weekly Gazette & Comet*:

> When the result was announced, there was such a shout as never before went up from the old Gothic Building. At this moment Capt. H. W. Allen walked in front of Gov. Moore, Col. Bragg, Rev. Mr. Linfield, Father Hubert, and other distinguished gentlemen, came down the central aisle bearing the glorious Pelican flag—the emblem of Independent Louisiana—which was received with waving of handkerchiefs by the daughters of Louisiana, and perfect hurricanes of applause from her gallant sons assembled. . . . A rocket went up from the State House grounds, which was the signal for raising the Pelican flag and the firing of guns.[3]

Following the vote to secede, the legislature adjourned for two weeks, giving everyone time to consider the momentous events. In spite of the recent legislative resolution, a concert by renowned singer Adelina Patti was scheduled for the State House. Tickets sold out, but, perhaps reflecting the mood and confusion of the people, almost no one actually attended the performance. A melancholy reporter for the *Weekly Gazette & Comet* seemed prophetic when he wrote, "Go where you may—the soft, sweet, gentle accents of 'Home' as you breathed it, will linger about the very stones of the old Capitol, when in the spirit of revolution it may lie in ruins."[4]

Uncertainty about the future soon yielded to active planning. The *Capitolian-Advocate* reminded the people of Baton Rouge of the numerous attempts to remove the capital from their city and urged residents not to be greedy in charging returning legislators for accommodations. "It must occur to every one, that it is highly important to the future development of Baton Rouge, that these people be treated well and not overcharged."[5]

The year 1862 was one of turmoil and destruction for Baton Rouge. In May, Union troops occupied the town and the State House. Gen. Thomas Williams of the Union army wrote,

> I have quartered one reg't. in the State House, a beautiful building with terraced grounds bordered with trees and flowers. In the rotunda of the State House stands a life size statue of Washington, by the sculptor Powers. And a sentinel has, by my orders, been placed over it to stand watch and ward night and day.[6]

Throughout the summer, frightened residents abandoned their homes to seek safety in outlying areas. Union soldiers occupied a few of the empty homes, and photographs taken by Andrew Lytle suggest other troops may have borrowed abandoned furniture for their tents.[7] Not even the State House was immune to scavengers. A chaplain in the United States army, J. F. Moors, mentioned the State House in a letter to his wife saying, "The interior had been sacked and desolated when our troops took possession here a year ago."[8]

A few months later, in August, a fierce battle destroyed a large portion of Baton Rouge and took many young lives on both sides. Following the conflict, Union troops abandoned the town for other battle sites. Upon their return in December, they found little resistance and easily reoccupied Baton Rouge. Most local men were fighting with the Confederate army in other locations, and their families had evacuated the devastated town. The State House was again used as a barracks by Union troops and as a prison for captured Confederate soldiers. On the fateful evening of Sunday, December 28, 1862, the State House was besieged by a different kind of enemy—fire. Smoke and flames rose from the east side of the building. Alarms sounded and fire engines responded. By nine o'clock that evening, the fire seemed under control, and it was believed that the greatest portion of the building would be spared. But before daybreak on Monday, December 29, the alarms rang again. Remnants of the initial fire had smoldered undetected in rafters and walls before breaking out again. This time, raging flames mercilessly destroyed the building's interior. Union officers and troops were commended for their efforts to extinguish the fire with the help of a few remaining citizens.[9]

Just three days later, Brig. Gen. C. Grover formed a special board of inquiry to investigate the cause of the fire. The board concluded the fire was accidental and was caused by accumulated grime in an unstable chimney. The report did not completely exonerate Union troops, saying the building was in the care of soldiers untrained in firefighting techniques. They were inexperienced and unaware of hidden dangers. Underscoring the obvious, the report ended with, "The final destruction of the interior of the building was complete."[10]

It was a monumental blow to Baton Rouge. What remained of the Louisiana Confederate government moved north along the Mississippi River as Union troops advanced, first to Opelousas, then to Shreveport. By 1864, all of Louisiana had fallen, and a new constitution in 1868 officially named New Orleans the state capital.

Baton Rouge was left with nothing but the great, white exterior walls of the State House hovering over the town like a ghost of the war, a constant reminder of the death and destruction suffered by the town. The formerly beautiful building and grounds were left unattended. The exotic landscaping, which had been such a source of pride, fell prey to vandals, loose livestock, and even townspeople trying to replenish their own neglected gardens. In 1864, the gates were closed and guarded, and a general cleanup began.[11] A year later, a reporter strolling through town was pleased to see signs of recovery in some of the shrubbery. He thought the building was still beautiful from a distance, even though it was scarred and cracked by battle.

In response to the destruction, the *Tri-Weekly Advocate* stated,

> As we stand looking on this pile of massy walls, the mind goes back to the many scenes that they have witnessed, and the memories of the dead whose voices have rung through these halls haunt the thoughts of the most casual spectator. . . . The walls are silent now, the clamor of applause and shouts of exultation that once floated through these windows upon the sleepy old town beneath will no more wake the quiet citizens from his meditations.[12]

That same year, the *Weekly Advocate* railed against Gov. Henry Clay Warmoth for naming a black man as keeper of the State House grounds. The gardens, planted under the direction of the beloved Civil War hero and governor Henry Watkins Allen, were called "sacred" by the people of the state. Having the gardens tended by "the Illinois prince of Voodoohism"[13] was perceived as an attempt to add insult to injury by the powerless people who had already suffered ruinous defeat.

However, in late 1865, the heart of Baton Rouge began to beat again, and melancholy was replaced by practicality. When the state legislature began to discuss building a new State House, the people of Baton Rouge were determined to have their say. They believed that no vote of the people had ever moved the capital from Baton Rouge to New Orleans and called for the legislature to investigate the stability of the burned capitol's walls , if not to rebuild, then at least to salvage materials. The Baton Rouge *Tri-Weekly Advocate* estimated the cost of building a new capitol could be up to one million dollars. On the other hand, restoring the old State House would cost only seventy-five thousand dollars, because inspectors found the remaining walls of the old Gothic building to be sound. Simply in the interest of economy to the state, it would surely be wise to rebuild in Baton Rouge.[14]

By December, plans for building a new state house had begun in earnest. A committee was appointed to determine the best location. A resolution was presented to the legislature requiring the committee to, at the very least, visit Baton Rouge and prepare a report outlining the cost of restoring the burned structure to its original state.[15] The resolution failed.

Once again, the New Orleans press would hear no talk of moving the capital. It dismissed the idea of frugality by pointing out one big problem—the Constitution of 1864 fixed the capital at New Orleans.[16] End of discussion. But it was only the beginning of the second round of battle between Baton Rouge and New Orleans as both vied to be named state capital.

In March 1871, the final chapter in the story of George Washington's statue unfolded. Before the fire of 1862, Gen. Benjamin Butler, commander of troops occupying the State House, wrote, "I have sent the statue of Washington to the mayor of New York, to be held in trust for the people of Louisiana until they shall have returned to their senses."[17] In 1865, the legislature asked for its return.[18] Instead, the statue was sent to Washington, D.C., where it was displayed at the United States Patent Office.[19] This theft greatly insulted Louisiana, and it was later called "the most outrageous act of spoilation that ever made an American cheek tingle with shame."[20] Following the Civil War, Gov. Henry Clay Warmoth and Sen. William Pitt Kellogg successfully sought the return of the statue to Louisiana. Its first public display was slated for the State Fair in New Orleans. The wooden building in which the statue was stored caught fire, but no water was available. In spite of the firemen's efforts, the battle was lost. The building and its contents, including the statue, were destroyed. Although the marble statue of George Washington just missed the destructive State House fire of 1862, it was not so lucky nine years later.[21]

Chapter Five

Returning to Baton Rouge

While in New Orleans during Reconstruction, the legislature conducted business in the leased Mechanic's Institute. There were occasional attempts to build a state house in New Orleans, but funds never seemed sufficient to accomplish construction. One of the most unusual proposals was to erect two separate but equally magnificent buildings on opposite sides of Canal Street. One would house the General Assembly, and the other would house the remainder of the state offices. A beautiful arched bridge over Canal Street would connect the two. The cost was estimated at four million dollars. Another almost successful proposal was to buy "a small plantation between New Orleans and Carrollton" and build a grand state house, also at a very high cost.[1]

In 1875, the St. Louis Hotel at the corner of Canal and Royal was offered for sale. The legislature, interested in larger quarters and a permanent home, provided for its purchase at $250,000 plus interest. Gov. William Kellogg vetoed the bill because the wording was confusing and the premium price with interest made for extremely high payments. Both houses of the legislature overrode the governor's veto, and the St. Louis Hotel became the property of the state and the new State House.[2] The old hotel served as the seat of state government for seven years. Still desiring a new capitol building, however, the legislature made a bold decision in early 1877. It authorized Louisiana's Congressional delegation to ask the United States government for funds to repair the State House in Baton Rouge. The building had, after all, been destroyed while occupied by the United States Army.[3] Of course, funds were never provided.

When Rutherford B. Hayes was elected president of the United

States, the iron grip of Reconstruction loosened. Many political factions fought for control of Louisiana's state government. At least one group felt that moving the legislature back to Baton Rouge would return Louisiana to the glory it had enjoyed before the Civil War. By 1878, serious attempts to move the state capital were underway. Wounds still fresh from the war and Reconstruction, as well as legislative corruption, finally began to sway public opinion in favor of removing the capital from New Orleans.

A Baton Rouge newspaper suggested that the majority of Louisiana's citizens were never consulted on the decision to move the capital to New Orleans in the first place. The paper argued that the capital had been moved at the point of a bayonet against the wishes of the people, and it should be returned to its rightful place in Baton Rouge.[4] The Baton Rouge and New Orleans presses once again began firing editorial volleys at one another. The Baton Rouge *Weekly Advocate* stressed the economy of rebuilding in Baton Rouge on property already owned and improved by the state. In addition, Baton Rouge pledged to donate twenty-five thousand dollars—or about one quarter of the estimated cost—towards reconstructing the State House.[5]

The New Orleans *Bee* said that removal would be a public calamity. It could not find so much as one good reason to pursue the proposal. After all, Baton Rouge had insufficient accommodations and no railroad. Sophisticated gentlemen would quickly tire of Baton Rouge and quit running for office, ensuring the election of inferior candidates. Of paramount importance to the *Bee* was the belief that the everyday press would find it hard to get information and investigate bills in order to warn the people about bad legislation. Measures could be adopted and enacted before the press could alert the public, rendering legislative sessions essentially secret.[6] The *Weekly Advocate* printed a point by point rebuttal of the *Bee*'s arguments. It added that railroads, hotels, and communications needed to be developed in all of Louisiana's cities, rather than concentrating them in one grand city.[7]

On July 4, 1878, a rally was held in bunting-draped Baton Rouge. Hundreds of people from the former capital and surrounding parishes enjoyed patriotic speeches, dancing on the State House grounds, and abundant refreshments prepared by the fair ladies of the city. Looming over the revelers, the empty walls of the burned capitol bore a large canvas sign with the painted message "For State Capital: Baton Rouge."[8]

A November election was scheduled to vote on constitutional amendments; first among them was the location of the state capital. Amendment No. 1 read:

> That the seat of Government shall be established at the city of Baton Rouge or at the city of New Orleans, as the majority of the voters of the State may determine at the next ensuing election: those voting to locate the State capital at Baton Rouge shall indorse on their tickets, 'For State Capital, Baton Rouge:' those voting to locate the capital at New Orleans shall indorse on their tickets, 'For State Capital, New Orleans.' (Strike out article one hundred and thirty-one.)[9]

The wording of the amendment caused so much confusion people feared the matter could only be decided in the state Supreme Court. Voters were supposed to vote "for the amendment," or "against the amendment." However, the wording tricked many people into writing "For State Capital, Baton Rouge" or "For State Capital, New Orleans," on their ballots. Of the ballots cast, Baton Rouge received a majority of over six thousand votes. The New Orleans *Democrat* asserted that those ballots not properly cast for or against the entire amendment should be declared invalid, as those voters "did not vote on the amendment intelligently."[10]

Every other proposed amendment was defeated, even though the people desired some of them. The public was in a nasty mood and wanted a new constitution, and by rejecting all the other amendments they hoped to force a constitutional convention.[11] In early 1879, a convention was indeed called. The *Louisiana Capitolian,* a newspaper created with the expressed purpose of returning the capital to Baton Rouge, was unmerciful to New Orleans. It challenged delegates to the constitutional convention to listen to the wishes of the people and move the capital back to Baton Rouge. One reporter wrote:

> Everybody remembers the extra sessions that have followed every assembling of the General Assembly since the war, the daily adjournments after two or three hours' sitting, the continued neglect to attend to the committee duties at night, by the members drawn as they were to the theatres and the alluring saloons of the Crescent City. As a result, the last two days of each session were impossible because bills were being rushed through at the last minute without the study or attention of legislators who barely had time to read their titles.[12]

A convention delegate from Orleans Parish proposed another election to decide the location of the capital. The move drew howls of protest from the Baton Rouge press, which, once again, felt the need to defend and extol the virtues of its city.[13] One newspaper quoted an editorial from the *Vicksburg Commercial,* which said, "New Orleans appears never to have developed the delight in the honor which a capital city is expected to experience."[14]

In an all-out effort to become the capital, Baton Rouge authorized its constitutional convention delegates to increase the original offer to thirty-five thousand dollars toward rebuilding the State House. The gesture paid off. In July, delegates to the constitutional convention voted overwhelmingly to locate the state capital in Baton Rouge, but one large stumbling block was placed in the way. It was stipulated that the money had to be collected and deposited with the state before any building contracts could be signed. This was a last, desperate effort by those who hoped Baton Rouge would be unable to raise the funds.[15]

Defending its city, the *New Orleans Democrat* fired off a sarcastic article saying Baton Rouge had surely prospered under its pretense of being a modest town. Just let the poor little town live. Please give it the capital, and it would ask for no more. After all, it didn't have much, just the Penitentiary, three state-supported schools for the handicapped, and the state college with law and medical schools.[16]

In spite of the incessant bickering, the constitution of 1879 named Baton Rouge the capital city of Louisiana. The city, which was expectedly delighted at the honor of being capital was once again ready to welcome state government and to rebuild the beloved, abandoned State House.

Chapter Six

Rebuilding the Castle

The citizens of Baton Rouge were euphoric. The *Louisiana Capitolian* declared, "The bells should ring with merry chimes when the first hand is laid in the glorious work of restoration."[1]

The legislature formed the Senate Joint Committee to Investigate the Condition of the State House at Baton Rouge and sent it to inspect the ruined building, determine needed repairs, and estimate the cost. The committee recommended removing all interior walls above the basement level and removing twenty-five to forty feet from the top of the exterior walls. Its most surprising recommendation was to change the design of James Dakin's building by capping it with a Mansard roof equipped with a dome. The committee was astonished to find a complete lack of "all necessary conveniences such as a water supply, water closets and heating." It recommended installing the plumbing necessary for these conveniences on each floor, with drainpipes leading to the river. The building was to be heated with steam. The estimate for repairs and improvements was $180,000.[2]

A bill providing funds to rebuild the State House passed the legislature in April 1880. The total appropriated was $176,000, with $141,000 due from the state and $35,000 from Baton Rouge.[3] Gov. L. A. Wiltz, Lt. Gov. Samuel McEnery, Sen. James Hagan, Gen. G. W. Munday, Mr. S. M. Robertson, Dr. T. J. Buffington, and Mr. F. L. Richardson were appointed as commissioners to oversee the restoration.[4]

By far, the most contentious member of the State House Commission was Senator Hagan of New Orleans, chairman of the Senate Committee on Public Buildings. At first, he supported the Mansard roof. Then in May of 1880, he asked for consideration of another design, this one with a dome over the building and a huge covered platform suitable for a "dancing party" on the roof.[5] After Hagan's ideas were dismissed, he attended subsequent meetings sporadically and was almost always highly critical of the proceedings.

The commission met Friday, May 14 to consider a plan submitted by architect William Freret. William Alfred Freret was a New Orleans native but received an engineering degree in England. By 1859, he had designed many buildings in his hometown, many of which made extensive use of cast iron. Later, he designed many federal buildings throughout the United States.[6] Freret's presentation to the commission, unlike Dakin's simple sketch, consisted of "elaborate drawings" of his proposed building.[7] He stayed true to the overall architectural flavor of Dakin's design, but he added several up-to-date necessities and decorative elements. Freret was appointed permanent architect.

Another item on the agenda of that May meeting was a report on the condition of the walls. It was prepared by men who had worked on the original State House from 1847 to 1850, and they believed that the walls were in good condition, except for a few cracks. They found no reason for the state to incur the expense of new walls when the old ones were almost as good as new.[8] Their recommendation was approved, and bids were called to build a new interior within the existing exterior. Wages and salaries were also set. Freret was to receive twenty-five hundred dollars per year as supervising architect. Thompson J. Bird, named superintendent under the architect, would receive two hundred dollars a month. The bricklayers' foreman, Mr. Brown, would be paid five dollars a day, and day laborers would earn seventy-five cents each day they worked.[9]

The thirty-five thousand dollars Baton Rouge had pledged was raised in only eight days, allowing the city to crow but disappointing those who had hoped the town would be unable to produce the promised amount.[10] True to its word, on June 21, 1880, Baton Rouge deposited the required funds in the state treasury in time for contracts to be signed.[11] The constitution allowed Baton Rouge to issue bonds of indebtedness, but the city was proud to announce it had raised cold, hard, cash money.[12]

On July 5, 1880, the State House Commission met in Baton Rouge, opened bids, and awarded contracts amounting to $55,710. Carpentry work was contracted for $22,000, and stone and marble work for $24,875. The contract for sand was eighteen hundred barrels at thirty-five cents per barrel. Bricks cost $9.75 per thousand.[13]

On July 29, the *Louisiana Capitolian* announced that construction had begun on the State House.[14] By late August, supplies were unloaded, debris was cleared, and the western towers were floored and roofed as offices for construction personnel.[15]

When the State House Commission met in August, most plans and bids were complete. The commission responded to an ongoing problem by appointing a three-man committee to address Commissioner Hagan's complaints. Fellow commissioners felt that they were being unfairly criticized and that the public was being purposefully misled.[16] The following day, the committee reported that Hagan's statements were not in accordance with the facts. It concluded that his problems with the commission began early on when he was not elected chairman and his plan was not adopted. It was also noted that he had not attended any commission meetings except the most recent since these setbacks.[17]

Work on the State House progressed slowly, hampered by incessant rain and, as with the original construction, late delivery or lack of materials. In late September, supports for the roofs of the two legislative chambers were placed. In October, makeshift stairs were built, and the public was allowed to roam the building and the promenade on its roof to see the progress being made.[18] However, an unusually rainy December almost completely stopped construction. On the few dry days, workers began tearing away the top of the building in order to comply with Freret's plan of adding a fourth story in the center of the building.[19]

January of 1881 brought more delays caused by rain and lack of materials, particularly ironwork for the rotunda. Freret's design included and expanded the decorative ironwork initially used by Dakin. In March, a large shipment of iron and flooring finally arrived by steamer from New Orleans. By then, the walls of the additional story over the center of the building were going up, and the building was declared "handsomer than before."[20] May brought hopes that the building would be sufficiently complete by fall to hold the legislature in the likely case that an extra session became necessary.

By summer, the legislative chambers were roofed and floored, and the rear gallery above the House chamber was almost complete. Window frames were placed in the first and second stories, and brick work neared completion. Painters, plumbers, gas-fitters, slaters, joiners, and coppersmiths swarmed throughout the building.[21]

Legal quarreling began when it seemed almost certain that an extra session of the legislature would be called for December. The Baton Rouge press demanded the session be held in Baton Rouge despite the fact that the State House was not yet finished. Because the constitution named Baton Rouge the capital, the question arose as to whether anything enacted by the legislature would be legal if that body met in New Orleans.

At the October meeting of the State House Commission, a few members argued that the building would be complete enough to receive the legislature by December. Mr. Hagan, true to precedent, complained that much of the work being done was "shoddy and unsubstantial," expenses were too high, and the work force was insufficient. It was noted that he was alone in his criticism.[22] In November, Commissioners Richardson and Robertson continued to advocate holding the session in the unfinished building, even though walls were not plastered, gas was not connected, permanent stairs were not in place, and scaffolding still occupied rooms. Fortunately, reason prevailed. Samuel Douglas McEnery, who had become governor in October at the death of Gov. Louis Wiltz, thought it would be dangerous to hold the session in Baton Rouge. He believed that what the legislature accomplished was more important than where it met, and the extra session was held in New Orleans.[23] One important act that passed during that session was the appropriation of funds necessary to complete the State House:

$126,302.17. This amount covered the previous appropriations of 1880 and 1881.

Even that seemingly innocuous proposal was the subject of heated controversy. The *New Orleans City Item* suggested the appropriation violated the constitution. Further, the paper called for judicial interference.[24] Judge N. H. Rightor took up the cause and issued an injunction claiming the appropriation was unconstitutional because it violated guidelines set up in the constitution. State House warrants were paid by preference, meaning they were among the first to be paid if tax revenues did not meet projections. That could leave other areas, including the judges's salary, short.[25]

The *Capitolian-Advocate* fired back that Judge Rightor's salary was also paid by preference and that the courts of New Orleans had no jurisdiction in this matter. The judge was trying to circumvent legislative action. By so doing, he would set a precedent, which meant that "every appropriation, every administrative measure, can be suspended by an injunction."[26] The *Weekly Capitolian-Advocate* suggested that the legislature impeach any judge who so blatantly interfered with its will.[27]

Many feared that construction on the State House would stop for lack of funds. However, in February the Citizen's Bank of Baton Rouge, trusting the state would correct any warrant problems, pledged to make advances in order for work to continue.[28] On March 1, Governor McEnery signed $126,000 worth of warrants, which were then deposited in the Citizen's Bank.[29]

In spite of all the legal wrangling, construction on the State House continued. In January of 1882, the State House Commission decided to accelerate work on the lower floors so they would be ready for the governor and state archives by March. A committee was appointed to plan for seven statues representing the history of the state to be placed in the rotunda, but the idea never went any further. It was announced that the central iron stairway would not be ready for the next legislative session. A proposal to erect a temporary staircase of wood was made but met with objection because of the expense.[30]

By the beginning of February, the first- and second-floor offices, as well as the House chamber, were plastered and painted. The mantelpieces were set, and the large windows dominating the House and Senate chambers were installed. The rooms were clean, light, and fresh.[31]

A shipment of legislators' desks and other small items from the St. Louis Hotel arrived on February 21. Other shipments of equipment and furniture arrived throughout the next few months.

When the time for the actual governmental transfer to Baton Rouge was at hand, the journalistic fight became downright nasty. The *Capitolian-Advocate* wrote that state officials would no longer be subjected to "the mellifluous atmosphere which they and their predecessors have breathed with more or less distended nostrils." Continuing the tirade, it stated, "New Orleans will cease to be the State of Louisiana, and become simply one of its integral parts." The *New Orleans Times Democrat* responded that Baton Rouge had described itself as an innocent, incorruptible city, but the same kinds of problems that had plagued New Orleans would quickly follow legislators to Baton Rouge "as a buzzard does the failing warhorse." Baton Rouge readily admitted it could not offer as much fun in an entire legislative session as New Orleans could in one day, but "it won't haunt them in the multiplicity of forms, in which it presents itself to them in the Crescent City."[32]

On February 24, the *Daily Picayune* reported the sounds of a funeral, tramping feet, and nails being hammered into wooden boxes as in a coffin. The sounds were the state government boxing up to be shipped on the steamboat *Edward J. Gay*. Many state employees were clearly dismayed at leaving New Orleans with its businesses and amusements.[33] Two days later, resigned to the inevitability of losing the capital, the same newspaper questioned whether the chemical composition of "the provincial puddle" was any purer than "the swamps of the metropolis," and whether rural honesty and morality were truly better than that of the great city.[34]

March 1 was a big day for everyone involved. On that day, Capt. L. Fremaux, Register of the State Land Office, resigned his office rather than move to Baton Rouge, because moving was more of a sacrifice than he was willing to make.[35] Governor McEnery and other state officers were not so pessimistic. They gathered in New Orleans early in the morning and crossed the Mississippi River by ferry to reach the railroad line on the west bank. Cannons boomed and well-wishers waved hats in the air as the party crossed the river. Once on the other side, officials boarded a special train bound for the new capital.[36]

The departure from New Orleans may have been somber, but the arrival at Baton Rouge was jubilant. No elaborate ceremony was planned, but an excited, spontaneous demonstration occurred as citizens from around the state gathered in anticipation of the state officials' arrival. Three companies of firemen, the Cadet Corps, two cannons, and a band also awaited them. The mayor, city councilmen, and prominent citizens of Baton Rouge ferried across the river shortly after noon to meet the train. Officials were ferried to the Baton Rouge side of the river, where they were greeted with booming cannons and music from the Silver Cornet Band. The honored guests boarded carriages and rode through Lafayette and Main Streets before arriving at the capitol. A few brief patriotic speeches were made before state officials took possession of their new offices.[37]

The celebration was marred by one unfortunate incident. Robert Harry, a young cannoneer, was severely injured when the cannon he was loading fired prematurely. Physicians attended to him immediately, but the "gallant" cannoneer lost an arm and had serious powder burns on his right eye and shoulder. A great outpouring of sympathy for the young man, injured in volunteer service to the city, resulted in a fund established for his benefit.[38] Several months later, the newspaper reported that Robert, who subsequently lost his right eye, was not content to be idle despite his great loss. He was selling valuable books and was praised as "a worthy man" with "a worthy business."[39]

Officials occupied the State House in March 1882, but the building was, in truth, far from finished. Building commissioners became short-tempered and demanded to know why work was not progressing more quickly. As of March 9, expenses totaled $106,666.23.[40]

Consequently, the pace of construction increased in order to have the chambers ready for the legislature in May. The front of the spectator's gallery in the House chamber was finished, at a cost of about $541 for both materials and labor. Water tanks were placed on the roof.[41] Chandeliers from the old St. Louis Hotel were polished and hung.[42] By the end of April, both chambers were nearly complete. The only work remaining in the House was to place the stained-glass panes in the windows behind the speaker's stand.[43] The *Capitolian-Advocate* gave the following descriptions.

> The Governor's office was . . . a model of chaste elegance. Tall ceilings beautifully frescoed, heavy paneled doors, and a beautiful mantel-piece carved out of snow white Vermont marble, together with its handsome furniture, give this a cosy and inviting appearance. . . . The [House] chamber is large, with a tall ceiling and the walls newly plastered. The desks and chairs for use of members are placed on an inclined floor; the floor being covered with a neat, new carpet. The visitors' gallery . . . is comfortably arranged over the main entrance. The Senate chamber, in the east end, will be arranged the same. . . . On Monday, everything will be ready for our law-makers."[44]

The declaration by local newspapers that the State House was almost complete was a positive spin on reality. Large portions of the building, notably the rotunda, were still unfinished. Nonetheless, the legislature convened in its new quarters in May of 1882. Governor McEnery addressed the gathered assembly. He attributed the delay in construction to problems with disposing of warrants and praised Citizen's Bank for its generous advances, which allowed construction to continue. McEnery surprised the gathering by recommending that the $35,000 Baton Rouge had donated for reconstruction be returned to the city. He did not like the implication that the location of the capital was a "matter of bargain." He said the voters of the state had moved the capital to Baton Rouge, and the required donation was a "hardship."[45] However, no evidence has been found that the money was ever returned.

Some legislators, finding themselves in Baton Rouge after almost twenty years in New Orleans, apparently did miss the big city. They were reportedly stumbling over themselves in a "helter-skelter foot race" to leave town. After voting themselves a shortened Friday session, they would catch the first ferryboat headed south and spend weekends forgetting their cares in the former capital city.[46]

By July, tall, iron turrets were in place on the eastern towers.[47] Black and white marble tiles were laid in a checkerboard pattern on the first floor of the rotunda.[48] In September, four of the six iron turrets were in place, and the remaining two were being erected. Some people liked their appearance, and some did not. Iron and stone work continued, as well as interior painting and flooring.[49]

It was about this time that Mark Twain, traveling on the Mississippi River, passed Baton Rouge on his way to New Orleans. In *Life on the Mississippi,* Twain's caustic description of the restored building said it was "pathetic" that such a castle was ever built in the first place. He could not understand why the "architectural falsehood" was being rebuilt and believed dynamite should have finished what the fire had begun.[50]

In the spring of 1882, beautiful white lions, originally located at the Royal Street entrance of the St. Louis Hotel in New Orleans, were moved to stand guard over state offices at the Baton Rouge State House. A local newspaper reported, "The ornaments for the new entrance at the State House, taken from the St. Louis Hotel, arrived here yesterday."[51] They were probably initially intended to guard the new, north entrance. However, in November, the *Weekly Capitolian-Advocate* reported a discussion about whether the lions should be moved from the east entrance to the west entrance, flanking the new stairs on the western terraces.[52] The lions, seemingly undisturbed by their odyssey, still rest at the top of the western stairs, where they can see and be seen from the Mississippi River.

Major construction continued for another sixteen months. Delays in the delivery of decorative iron for the rotunda produced months of waiting. Portions of the tile floors did not arrive until April 1883.[53] In May, work continued on the north entrance, but then work stopped completely until another shipment of iron was delivered in September.[54]

Only casual mention is made of the magnificent, spiral staircase in the center of the rotunda. Thirty-two steps, each over six feet long, fan out from the center column directly under the stained-glass dome and rise to the second-floor gallery. In October of 1883, the *Daily Capitolian-Advocate* noted simply, "The iron stairs have been completed."[55] Six months later, craftsmen fashioned a hand rail for the spiral staircase.[56]

The year 1884 started on a bad note. A water tank on the roof over the north entrance leaked and damaged much of the plaster in that area of the building.[57] Between then and the end of April, workmen finished the grand, new north entrance and the breathtaking ruby, gold, and azure stained-glass dome over the rotunda. There was no grand celebration or dedication at the end of construction. State officials had occupied their offices for at least a year, and legislators had already met in their new chambers. In May, Governor McEnery was inaugurated on a stand decorated with greenery, flowers, and patriotic banners. The stand was erected on the northeast corner of the grounds under the lush foliage of massive magnolias and live oaks.[58]

The commissioners who had overseen the reconstruction of the State House turned the completed building over to the state in the summer of 1884.[59] The architectural integrity of James Dakin's castle remained relatively intact under William Freret's restoration, but there were a few significant changes. A fourth floor with six new offices was added to the center of the building. A huge, stained-glass dome was installed over the rotunda to alleviate the dark interior, and a glassed-in room called a lantern was built around it. Townspeople welcomed the addition of a grand entrance on the north side, which led them to the splendid spiral staircase in the center of the rotunda. Tall iron towers atop the east and west towers, and smaller turrets atop each corner, added architectural interest, but often invited ridicule. Last, but certainly not least, was the color of the exterior. Instead of the glistening white of Dakin's day, the building was painted a dark, brick red with light trim. The final cost of rebuilding the State House, about $180,000, was exactly the original estimate.

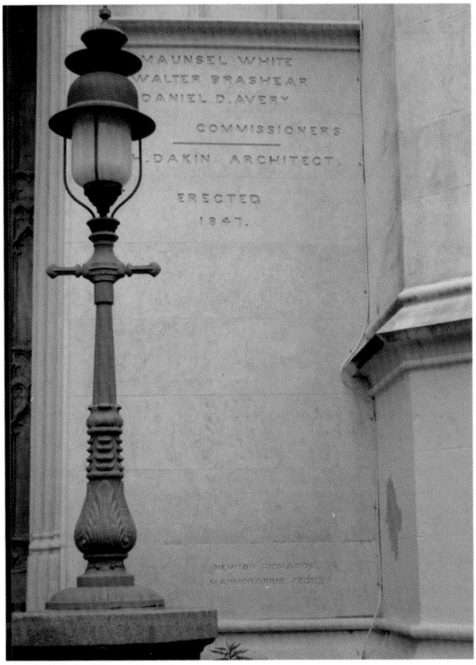

Names of original building commissioners White, Brashear, and Avery, and architect James Dakin, are engraved in marble at the west entrance.

Workmen adding iron towers and turrets, a fourth floor, and a lantern (housing for the stained-glass dome) pose atop the state house during the reconstruction that occurred from 1880 to 1882. (Courtesy Andrew D. Lytle Photograph Collection, Mss #893, Louisiana and Lower Mississippi Valley Collections, LSU Libraries, Baton Rouge, LA)

Engraving shows Union soldiers placing the American flag atop the towers of the Louisiana State House following occupation in 1862. (Published in The Soldier in Our Civil War, *1885)*

The State House lies abandoned with its interior in ruins after an accidental fire while occupied by Union troops in 1862. (Courtesy Andrew D. Lytle Photograph Collection, Mss #3708, Louisiana and Lower Mississippi Valley Collections, LSU Libraries, Baton Rouge, LA)

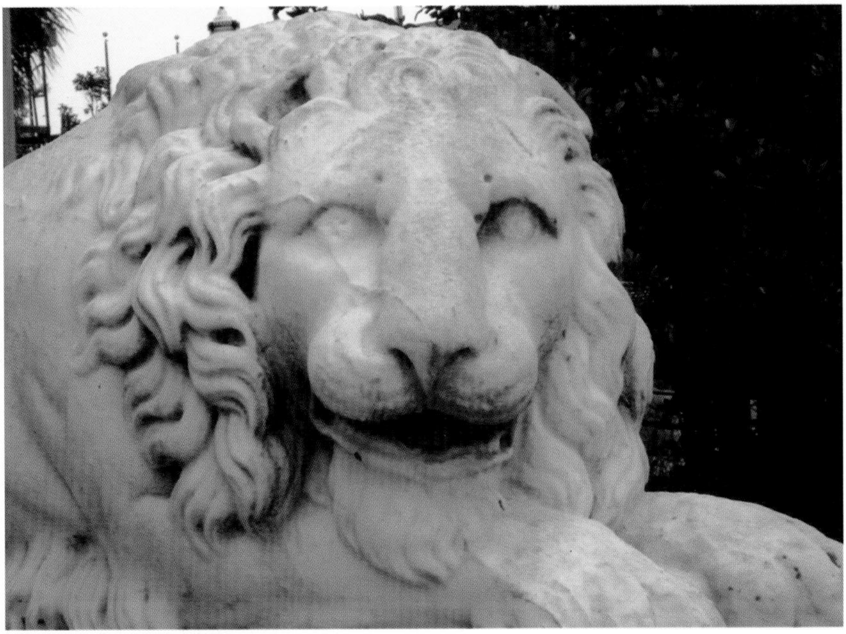

One of a pair of lions moved from the St. Louis Hotel in New Orleans rests atop the terrace stairs at the western entrance.

Tall iron towers and turrets were added, and the State House was painted dark red following Freret's 1880s restoration. (Courtesy Andrew D. Lytle Photograph Collection, Mss #3708, Louisiana and Lower Mississippi Valley Collections, LSU Libraries, Baton Rouge, LA)

The bust of Gov. Francis T. Nicholls was kidnapped as a prank but was returned and now stands in the rotunda.

A stained-glass window rises almost two stories in the House chamber. A similar window stands in the Senate chamber.

A magnificent stained-glass dome fans out four stories above the rotunda.

In a modern restoration of the exterior, all windows, including this quatrefoil window, were stripped of paint to expose the iron frames. Plaster was removed from the walls revealing bricks covered since the 1850s.

The seven-foot tall cast iron fence, built with interlocking pieces, was completed in 1855 and surrounds the entire grounds.

A monument rests over the burial site of Gov. Henry Watkins Allen who was interned on the State House grounds in 1885.

An unusual ginkgo tree, the only one remaining of three planted on the grounds of the State House, was brought to the United States by H. W. Allen while he served in the legislature in the 1860s.

The inauguration of Samuel Douglas McEnery in 1884 was held under the massive oaks on the northeast corner of the grounds. (Courtesy Andrew D. Lytle Photograph Collection, Mss #893, Louisiana and Lower Mississippi Valley Collections, LSU Libraries, Baton Rouge, LA)

This boxcar, one of forty-nine given to the United States by France following World War II, was placed on the State House grounds following distribution of the gifts inside.

Chapter Seven

Good Times and Bad

The years between 1884 and 1908 were ones of relative tranquility for the State House. Following Gov. Samuel Douglas McEnery's inauguration in 1884, the legislature settled into its newly rebuilt home. Periodically, state officials saw fit to beautify and modernize the building and grounds, but after the turn of the century, rumblings of dissatisfaction with the aging building began to surface.

In 1884, the legislature acted to honor Henry Watkins Allen, beloved Confederate governor from 1864 to 1865. Fearing reprisals after the Civil War, Allen went into exile in Mexico, where he died a year later. His body was eventually brought to New Orleans and buried in Lafayette Cemetery No. 1. Many people still harbored strong feelings for the Confederate general and believed internment on the State House grounds would be a more lasting and fitting memorial. The reburial occurred on July 4, 1885, with great pomp and ceremony. A lavishly decorated stand was erected on the northeast corner of the grounds under the shade of oak and magnolia trees. The program included speeches, prayers, poetry readings, and processions. Hoping for a good view of the proceedings, men, women, and children filled the grounds and north windows of the State House. The monument originally erected over Allen's grave in New Orleans had been moved and reset on the north side of the upper terrace, where it awaited his remains. He was buried beneath the monument with dignity and honor before the huge crowd that had come to pay him tribute. The monument still stands by the northwest corner of the building, overlooking the lower grounds and the Mississippi River.[1]

In 1900, the House chamber reverberated with the voice of William Jennings Bryan, former congressman, renowned orator, and presidential nominee. Following the speech, he was the guest of honor at a lovely reception held in the first-floor governor's suite, which had been tastefully decorated by the ladies of Baton Rouge.[2]

Despite occasional attempts at maintenance, neither the building nor the grounds received regular upkeep or proper care. In 1892, the *Daily Advocate* reported that the shabby appearance of the grounds reflected on the building and the state as a whole. The State House looked like a "noble ruin," which was admirable in its antiquity, but did not represent Louisiana's industry, heritage, or resources. The editor called for a commission to superintend the necessary maintenance.[3] A year later, the grounds were under the care of Mr. A. C. Blount, who was seen cutting the grass with a new lawn mower. It was such an exciting innovation that even Gov. Murphy J. Foster "came out and gave the new machine a few rounds and pronounced it a success."[4]

In March of 1893, a pond, or "aquarium," was drained so it could be rebuilt as a concrete pool with a fountain in the center. Constructed in the 1850s on the lower terrace of the southwestern grounds, the pond was about forty feet in diameter. The draining caused quite a public stir, and crowds of spectators came to watch. Their interest lay not so much in the fountain as in the local whisperings that, during the Civil War, some residents of the city had used the pond to hide valuable silver and jewels rather than have them fall into the hands of Union soldiers.[5]

The curious crowd was not disappointed. When most of the water had been drained, items that had been hidden at the bottom and covered with mud for years were revealed. A large box containing twenty-five Colt infantry rifles, complete with bayonets, was among the first items retrieved. Another large box contained a complete silver service bearing the initials "N. G." Yet another held old bank notes and bonds, probably hidden by someone hoping to reclaim his wealth after the war. A brass wire was strung with some long-forgotten lady's jewelry, rings of topaz and rubies, and a diamond solitaire of five to seven karats. A tin tag, which presumably had contained the name of the owner, was attached to the jewelry, but after years in the mud, it was no longer legible. A beautiful sword and silver spurs believed to have belonged to Federal soldiers were also found. Other items ranged from old tools and ammunition to a sausage grinder and hoop skirt. Without doubt, the discovery that caused the most commotion was that of a human skeleton. No hints remained as to who it was or how it got there, but authorities said it was "not beyond possibility that it will lead to the unearthing of some dark crime and may yet unearth a foul murderer."[6]

The pond was not the only State House beautification project Baton Rouge considered. Even the old iron fence constructed in 1855 had been subjected to criticism, and its removal was debated. As Baton Rouge grew, the town council passed ordinances prohibiting free-roaming livestock. Because the tall, iron fence no longer needed to protect the State House grounds from the hooves and appetites of livestock, the *Daily Advocate* called for it to be reduced to no more that two feet in height and landscaped with pretty flowers and shrubs.[7] In 1902, an anonymous citizen suggested removing the fence altogether, selling it, and using the proceeds to beautify the grounds.[8] Fortunately, the suggested improvements were not carried out.

The legislature did take advantage of modern inventions, and in 1894 it appropriated $1,086 to wire the State House for electricity.[9] The reconstruction commissioners of 1880 may have been surprised at the lack of necessary conveniences, but apparently they did little to rectify the situation. The legislature of 1896 called for the addition of indoor urinals, water closets, and washrooms on three floors as well as the necessary sewer connections.[10] In 1899, ten thousand dollars was appropriated for the purchase and installation of an elevator and renovation of some offices.[11] The first elevator was installed in the southeast corner of the rotunda in 1900.[12]

After almost twenty years of piecemeal maintenance, the building was indeed in need of a major overhaul, and in 1902, the legislature appropriated twenty-five thousand dollars for that purpose. For the next six months, workmen tried to reclaim the State House from years of neglect. The most obvious change was made to the exterior of the building. When rebuilt after the war, it had been painted a muted brick red. Much to the delight of the public and press, painters returned the building to its original white with "stone trimmings."[13] Exposed electric wiring and plumbing pipes were replaced and covered. All gas and electric light fixtures were replaced, except the finer ones, which were reworked and rehung. The north entrance was remodeled, and new oak doors were placed at the east and west entrances. Interior doors were refurbished, some with glass panels, and rehung. All interior woodwork was "grained to represent quarter oak."[14]

Though the years of 1884 through 1906 were fairly calm for Louisiana politics, some unusual political shenanigans did play out in the halls of the restored building. In 1896, Gov. Murphy J. Foster, a Democrat, ran for a second term against Republican John N. Pharr. Foster won the election, but hard feelings between the two camps created a volatile situation, which almost got out of hand. Republicans called for people to gather in Baton Rouge, hoping their show of support would force the legislature to investigate the vote. The move backfired when a flood of Democrats, many with firearms, arrived in Baton Rouge. Just days before the inauguration, three Republicans and a mass of Foster supporters crowded the rotunda and halls of the capitol. Outside the building, a shot rang out. Suspecting the worst, the Democrats indoors drew their guns, declared themselves deputy sheriffs, and surrounded the Republicans. The three Republicans were ordered to leave even though it was determined that the shot was accidentally fired when an unnamed Democrat dropped his gun.[15] The legislature voted overwhelmingly to dismiss any protest, and Foster was inaugurated a few days later on the grounds beneath the blooming magnolias.[16]

As the legislature prepared to meet in 1902, rumors of attempts to relocate the capital again surfaced. A trial-balloon was sent up proposing a new capitol at Audubon Park in New Orleans. It was presented as a plan to enhance the park and add dignity to Tulane University. As usual, the *Daily Advocate* responded by extolling the virtues of Baton Rouge, saying legislators would find wonderful new accommodations, streets, utilities, and public buildings in the capital city. The proposal died from the rest of the state's lack of interest.[17]

As if unable to thrive on good times, the State House sustained another blow that nearly destroyed it in 1906. On June 8, a fire of unknown origin broke out and severely damaged the Senate chamber. The fire was noticed at 1:00 A.M. by *Picayune* reporters finishing their stories after late-night legislative committee meetings. Within a few minutes, townspeople and legislators, some still in their nightclothes, rushed to the grounds. Many ran into the burning building to move vital records to the safety of the grounds and nearby residences. The roof over the Senate chamber was destroyed. Its furnishings were also destroyed, with the exception of one desk—Senator Stuckey rushed into the burning room and emerged a few seconds later with his desk in his arms. The damaging blaze was attributed to faulty electrical wiring in the attic between the towers above the Senate chamber, although it was rumored that a legislator may have left a smoldering cigar after a late night meeting.[18]

An assessment the next morning revealed that fire damage was contained to the Senate chamber. Fortunately, a large fireproof safe in that room protected vital Senate records. The floor and walls of the chamber, though damaged, were intact. Portraits of Governor Nicholls and General Beauregard hanging on the east walls of the Senate were destroyed. A large, valuable painting, "The Battle of New Orleans," and a portrait of Governor Foster hung on the west wall, and both survived the fire with minimal damage.

Offices below the Senate chamber received extensive water damage. State officers whose records had been removed during the fire spent the morning searching for them. Though totally disrupted in its routine, the legislature still met the day of the fire, the Senate in the nearby Istrouma Hotel, and the House in its regular chamber. The estimate for repairs was twenty-five thousand dollars.[19] The Baton Rouge Fire department received lavish praise for its efforts and was credited with saving the building. The legislature recognized its bravery with a donation of five hundred dollars to the department for its "valuable services."[20]

At the legislative session mere hours after the fire, while the ashes were still warm, legislators "stampeded" to present bills moving the capital from Baton Rouge to New Orleans and building a new capitol, estimated to cost two million dollars. Even the *Picayune* admitted there was no serious threat of removal but warned it would not be long before Louisiana needed a new State House, and it would be up to Baton Rouge to show why the capital should remain there.[21]

Contracts for repairs to the Senate wing of the State House were signed the next January. At first, it seemed that the square, southeast tower would have to be torn down and rebuilt, because it had cracked with the heat of the fire. Upon further inspection, it was discovered that the method of installing the huge iron cupolas atop each tower was causing the structural damage. All the towers posed a serious threat to the building and to anything below them. They were all removed, thus saving the south tower and preventing further structural damage to the others.[22] A contractor was paid to remove them and was allowed to keep any money he made by selling them as scrap iron.[23] Public opinion was mixed on the appearance of the building without the towers Mark Twain had mocked.

In July of 1907, new chandeliers were hung in the Senate to replace those destroyed in the fire. Light fixtures at the base of the stairs were also replaced, because the old ones were broken off when firemen rushed to extinguish the blaze. New ones, made of brass and of period design, were installed and fitted with arc lights.[24]

Repairs were complete enough for the Senate to meet in extra session in October of 1907, but the chamber was not finished.[25] As late as February of 1908, more than a year and a half after the fire, workmen were still putting finishing touches on the cavernous Senate chamber. Specifications called for "quarter-sawed, golden-finish oak," the same material as the new desks and chairs. Much to the delight of reporters, desks and "comfortable provisions" were included for them as well.[26]

"The Battle of New Orleans," the painting by Eugene Lami, which had hung in the Senate chamber, suffered smoke and water damage during the fire. The twelve-by-thirteen-foot painting was so large it had to be removed from its frame in order to be taken out of the charred room. For a short time, it was displayed in the House chamber. Before the fire, the legislature had haggled over ownership of the painting. Originally, it had hung in the old St. Louis Hotel, which served as State House when the capital was in New Orleans. When the capital moved to Baton Rouge, the painting was packed and shipped with the rest of the furnishings. Some felt the painting should be returned to New Orleans, but a measure to that effect was rejected by the legislature. After the fire, the director of the newly formed state museum approached Gov. Newton Blanchard with an interesting proposal. Because no public funds were available to restore the valuable painting, the state museum offered to restore it at no cost to the state. In return, the painting would remain in New Orleans, and the matter of ownership would be taken up at the next legislature. The offer was accepted. Although no evidence was found in legislative records that the matter was ever discussed, the painting remains in New Orleans on display at the Cabildo.[27]

Once again, the State House returned to life after a serious fire. But a powerful political storm was forming, and it would have a greater impact on the building's future than anyone could have realized.

Chapter Eight

Peace to Pandemonium

Compared to the whirlwind of activity after the fire, the years following 1908 were only a mild breeze fanned by undercurrents of important things to come. Huey Long was about to become governor—the old castle was about to experience excitement the likes of which it had never seen before. Thoughts of a new, modern state house were also forming, and it was the beginning of the end of government in the Gothic castle.

Not long after its installation in 1900, the elevator began to malfunction. It was often out of order, and repairs were costly. In 1906, inspectors condemned it after discovering a frayed cable.[1] Foot-weary legislators were forced to use the stairs until 1917, when a new elevator was installed at a cost of just under six thousand dollars.[2]

A year after fire-damage repairs were complete at the State House, another disaster struck. In the early morning hours of May 31, 1909, a severe storm hit Baton Rouge. A large portion of the roof above the dome was blown away, and strong winds ripped ladders from the top of the building. Wind-driven rain soaked the top three floors and the House chamber, but repairs were made quickly.[3]

In 1910, wires for telephone, telegraph, and electricity were placed underground. Removing the unsightly telephone poles and cables stretched across the State House grounds allowed an unobstructed view of the beautiful building. The *Daily State-Times* called for the removal of the fence as the only other improvement needed.[4]

Of course, legislative sessions during this period would not have been complete without the incessant aggravation of the removal question—once again, some wanted to move the capital away from Baton Rouge. This time, however, the antagonist was not New Orleans but Alexandria. In 1914, a delegation from Alexandria spoke before a packed Senate chamber about the merits of their city: its central location, railroads, and new luxury hotel. In order to get the measure passed and on a statewide ballot, they offered an unspecified site for a new capitol at no cost, and a half-million dollars towards construction.[5] The Alexandria Chamber of Commerce invited members of the House to board a special train bound for the central Louisiana city to inspect sites for the proposed state capitol. Taken by surprise, the Baton Rouge delegation asked for a delay and appointed a committee to formulate opposition to the measure. Opponents of the move accused the Alexandria legislative delegation of swapping votes on the capital removal issue for votes on a racehorse gambling bill that New Orleans wanted.[6] Emotions were close to the surface during the final debate about whether to place the constitutional amendment on the ballot. Alexandria delegates objected to the horde of Baton Rouge citizens who packed the House chamber in an attempt to influence votes. All townspeople, with the exception of the ladies, were asked to leave. Speakers from other towns objected to the bid from Alexandria, declaring that if the location of the capital were to be determined by the highest bid, the auction should be open to other towns as well. Bogalusa would offer one million dollars. Just as a vote was about to be taken, Judge Favrot of Baton Rouge moved to table the motion, effectively killing it. The vote to table passed 69 to 45.[7] The fight for a new location might have been over for the time being, but it underscored, in a very public way, the growing desire for a new, modern capitol building.

The threat of removing the capital grew tedious for legislators from Baton Rouge. It became a bargaining chip for causes proposed by any delegation. Each time a controversial political issue arose, Baton Rouge delegates were approached in hopes of trading their votes for reassurance the capital would not be moved. Local reporters, tired of the situation, said Baton Rouge had paid for the capital once and should not have to keep paying at every legislative session. The *State Times* suggested, "The next man who brings up the subject as a political threat should be politely told to go where there is no community swimming pool."[8]

As expected, during the legislative session of 1922, other cities put in their bids to win the title of state capital, but none of the assaults on Baton Rouge was strong enough to get the measure placed on a ballot. The building, which Dakin had believed adequate for the foreseeable future, was aging and proving too small for an expanding government. The tax commission and the highway commission were forced to rent offices in Baton Rouge. The Supreme Court, conservation department, fire marshal, and others had already moved to New Orleans in search of adequate office space.[9] Proponents of Baton Rouge mentioned that if a new capitol building were needed, the city could offer the site of the university in just a few years.[10] That location was about one mile north of the old State House and is, in fact, where the "new" capitol stands.

In the first part of the 1900s, the effects of World War I touched everyone in America. Patriotic citizens throughout the country were asked to do their part to conserve resources, especially food. In response, Louisiana's Commissioner of Agriculture planted barley, wheat, and sweet potatoes on the State House lawn. The demonstration garden was to prove that crops could be grown successfully in this climate and to encourage Louisiana landowners to follow suit.[11]

In another war-related effort, a benefit dance was staged on the grounds in 1918. About four hundred people attended the dance, and hundreds more watched from the terraces. The benefit raised two hundred dollars, which was contributed to the Soldiers and Sailors' Service Club.[12]

In 1920, the State House grounds were the scene of a rally promoting the women's suffrage movement. Women of all ages participated in a grand pageant advocating ratification of a constitutional amendment that would give women the right to vote. Local children held banners reading, "Give our mothers the ballot. It means better babies." A mock funeral was held for the seven sins, represented by members of the legislature, while beautiful women represented the virtues. "Asthetic" dancing concluded the program.[13]

An amazing, time-saving innovation was introduced in the legislative session of 1922. The Universal Indicator Company installed an electronic voting machine in the House chamber. Representatives loved it and cheered when a bill was introduced to negotiate for its purchase. It was evidently needed, because legislators often tried to shout each other down during voice votes, and roll call votes were time consuming. During one spirited debate, the speaker of the House broke his gavel trying to maintain order.[14]

That session earned the distinction of being the worst since Reconstruction. The *State Times* called it a three-ring circus with do-nothing legislators who whooped and hollered, threw paper balls, and engaged in fist fights. A reporter said he

> heard a guy ask the elevator boy if they used the Marquis of Queensbury rules in stagin' the bouts on the floor of the house. He said they had to call off the bouts on account of the boxing commission gettin' sore because the house didn't pay no license for the boxing affairs.

"Rocky Stewart" and "Kid Claiborne" were combatants in a fight stopped by fellow legislators when Claiborne's eyeglasses chipped the varnish off some furniture as he fell. It was called a misunderstanding, and apologies followed.[15]

In 1928, during the last days of Gov. Oramel H. Simpson's administration, the committee to investigate housing for state offices released its report. Several proposals were presented. One suggestion was to build two wings or annexes to the present structure; however, ground space was inadequate, and the architecture could not be designed to complement the current building. Another possibility was erecting a separate building to the east of the State House and connecting the two with an underground tunnel. That idea was dismissed, partly because of the cost, but primarily because it would forever erase the dream of a modern state house. After studying several plans, the committee agreed that a new state house was the only reasonable solution to the space shortage. They unanimously recommended building a new, modern state house at the site of the old university.[16] Although the need for a new structure was apparent to all, money was just not available, and a new capitol building was not a pressing political issue.

The *State Times* reported in 1928 that the old Gothic structure was in polished, perfect condition to greet the governor and the new legislature. Voting machines were placed in order, and dust, which had accumulated for at least a decade, was cleaned from every surface. Molding and windows got a thorough cleaning with soap and water.[17] The stage was set, and the curtain was about to rise on the debut of Gov. Huey Pierce Long.

Long's political star had risen quickly. During his campaign, he acknowledged the need for a new State House, but it was not a major campaign issue. Although Long had tremendous support from rural areas, he was not as well regarded in the cities. He was, nonetheless, elected governor in 1928 and inaugurated outdoors on the north side of the building. Thousands of spectators packed the grounds and nearby streets to get a glimpse of the proceedings. Many climbed the iron fence, hoping for a better view. People of all ages—men, women, children, blacks, and whites—braved the summer sun to get a glimpse of Long and to hear him take the oath of office. Following the official ceremonies, a cannon boomed in salute to the new governor as supporters tossed their hats into the air and shouted, "Long live Huey."[18]

The State House, although polished and perfect for the opening of legislative session, began to show its age and required Long's attention immediately. Ten iron turrets built at the top corners of the building during the 1880s reconstruction began to crumble. Governor Long ordered them removed after a large chunk, estimated at three hundred pounds, broke off and fell to the ground. The slate roof, which had leaked since construction, was replaced with one of tin, which was painted bright red and could be seen for miles.[19]

In a scathing political diatribe against Long, John K. Fineran wrote that Long had been overheard having a conversation with an insurance salesman about the State House a few months into his administration: "'Get the hell out of here with your proposition. I wouldn't give four thousand dollars for the whole damn building. I wish it was burned down, and any man that will burn it down I will see that he is not prosecuted.'"[20]

Long soon found himself fighting for his political life, leaving him no time to worry about the problems of an aging state house. In March of 1929, he called a special session to enact an occupational license tax aimed at large oil refineries. When it became apparent the legislation would not pass, he tried to adjourn the session and call another in two weeks. Opponents of the tax measure were determined not to let the session adjourn until the question had been resolved. Long's handpicked speaker, J. E. Fournet, refused to entertain any motion except adjournment. The House erupted in pandemonium as Rep. Cecil Morgan, shielded by friends and screaming out charges, moved to the podium. Ignoring all the commotion, Fournet ordered a vote for adjournment. The electronic machine recorded enough "aye" votes to adjourn. "At that a literal, not a figurative riot burst out." Rep. Clinton Sayes jumped over the speaker's desk and climbed a ladder leading to the voting machine operator, who admitted the machine malfunctioned. Nevertheless, Fournet declared the session adjourned. Angry representatives, determined to stay in session, stormed the podium. At least one legislator was seriously injured as the group was literally beaten back by Long's friends brandishing brass knuckles. Other skirmishes broke out on the floor.

Finally one disgusted legislator, Rep. Mason Spencer, made his way to the front of the room and shouted to be heard above the chaos. "In the name of decency and common justice!" In the hush that ensued, he called for a revote on adjournment. This time, the motion failed. The *Morning Advocate* reported that he spoke barely above a whisper but was easily heard in the quiet, "for everyone—members and spectators alike—realized that a new page in the state's history was being written."[21]

Talk of impeachment began to circulate. Long's friends busied themselves away from the capitol. The governor could often be seen alone as even his friends began to distance themselves from him.[22] Within days, several motions for the impeachment of Huey Long were filed.

Once again, Long tried to force the House to adjourn before the articles of impeachment could be introduced. The proceedings in the House attracted so many spectators that the building commissioner was asked to inspect the gallery for safety. He recommended a limit of 120 visitors.[23] In April 1929, the House voted to impeach Long and sent the charges to the Senate. One week later, two mysterious fires were extinguished at the State House. Both were discovered in the basement and were believed to be arson. The first fire started in old chairs and papers beneath the office where the governor's records were kept. The second fire began in paper taken from old books. In both instances, the alert night watchman smelled smoke and extinguished the fires. Rumors spread that he would lose his job in spite of his heroic effort, because he should not have allowed the fires to get started in the first place. Local insurance agents reported that Governor Long had refused to renew the old building's insurance policy when it expired just one month before the fires.[24]

At the end of April 1929, the Senate summoned Long to face charges. Just as that body convened to begin the trial, fifteen senators presented a document saying they would never vote for impeachment regardless of the evidence, effectively assuring a favorable outcome for the governor. Impeachment proceedings were cancelled, and Long remained in office.

Once back on strong ground, Long proposed many ambitious, costly programs for Louisiana, requiring new sources of revenue. Sen. J. L. Anderson, a Long supporter, proposed the issuance of five million dollars in bonds to build a new state capitol in Baton Rouge. The move was widely believed to be an effort to win approval from Baton Rouge legislators for Long's expensive highway program.[25] Other appealing offers were made to Shreveport and New Orleans. Both cities turned them down, considering them bribes.[26]

Baton Rouge was divided on the proposition of a new capitol. Although wanting the capital to remain in their city, Baton Rouge legislators were not willing to be pawns in Long's scheme. Funding for many of Long's ambitious programs was finally proposed as a constitutional amendment. During debate, everyone was reminded that the capital could still be moved from Baton Rouge. Long himself spoke about the old building, saying it was about to fall down, and there was nothing left to patch. He said there wasn't another building in the whole country that was such a disgrace and that he wouldn't pay twenty-five dollars for the whole thing.[27]

When it became apparent Long's forces would not get the two-thirds vote necessary to submit a constitutional amendment, they proposed, instead, a constitutional convention, believing that measure required only a simple majority vote.[28] Once again, Long took drastic measures to ensure the proposal would pass. His supporters would not allow the session to adjourn for the weekend, saying the governor's orders were to keep the legislature in town and the House in session. Long also appeared in person, intimidating legislators into keeping their seats and occasionally physically blocking the door as members attempted to leave.[29] The next day, angry legislators demanded that Long leave the floor and take his gunmen with him. Doors to the House chamber were then locked as heated debate continued.[30] By mid July, the constitutional convention bill died in the Senate, and Long's schemes were quashed for a time.

Later that month, Long announced his candidacy for the United States Senate, and he was elected in September 1930. Almost immediately, undenied rumors began to circulate that he would run for president of the United States. Feeling he had regained his power, Long called another special session of the legislature to prepare a constitutional amendment to fund his programs. This time the measure easily passed both houses. In November of 1930, the amendment was ratified, and the days of government in the grand old castle were near an end.

Once the decision to abandon the Gothic State House had been made, feelings of nostalgia for the old building began to surface. Newspapers throughout the state printed histories of construction, tales of intriguing legislative sessions, and speculation about the future of the building. A writer for the *Times Picayune* eloquently, and quite appropriately, stated, "It is a story of great men, magnificent gestures, political entanglements and war."[31]

The elegant old building was not destined to go down quietly and was the scene of one last, undignified fight. During the troubled times of Huey Long's reign as governor, Lt. Gov. Paul Cyr often spoke emotionally against him. When Long was elected to the U. S. Senate, he vowed to stay in Louisiana and finish his term as governor. He wanted to see his programs completed, but more importantly, he refused to let his bitter enemy Lieutenant Governor Cyr finish his term. When Long was called to fill his seat in the U. S. Senate in January of 1932, he named A. O. King, the president *pro tempore* of the Senate, to fill his term as governor. Both King and Cyr took the oath of office, but, aided by armed guards placed in and around the capitol and other state buildings to ward off Cyr, King had already occupied the governor's mansion and capitol offices.[32] Cyr's attempt to become governor failed, and King remained in office.

In 1932, construction on the new skyscraper capitol was complete. On May 9, the legislature convened for the last time in the Old State House and then adjourned without conducting any business. The next Monday, legislators gathered at the new capitol for the inauguration of Alvin O. King and held their first meeting in the new building. There was no closing ceremony or farewell for the old capitol. The building closed quietly, but people began to realize just how much a part of their lives the Old State House had become. An editor for the *State Times* wrote:

> There is a romance about the medieval castle. Its spiral stairway, its high embrasures, its turrets, the iron fence enclosing its grounds all speak of another day. . . . The old statehouse has been long outgrown. Yet it has become such an inseparable part of the life of Louisiana and of Baton Rouge that scarcely can one imagine it's no longer performing its usual functions. . . . After all, one cannot create the old—only the passing of Father Time can make traditions and store up memories, and give the charm that hovers about things rare and ancient.[33]

On a more practical note, people also realized that the new

capitol building secured the capital for Baton Rouge. The question of capital removal, which had consumed countless hours and days of almost every legislative session, was finally over.

Today, the quiet dignity of the legislative hall stands in sharp contrast to the tumultuous sessions once held in its cavernous chambers.

Chapter Nine

Abandonment

The people of Louisiana could hardly contain their excitement at the modern, thirty-two-story capitol, which seemed to touch the sky. Just as the old, abandoned capitol had its inspiring and stormy stories, the new one would have its stories too—including the assassination of Huey Long, the governor who presided over its construction.

With attention focused on the new building, the Old State House languished in neglect. An apartment was created on the third floor to provide quarters for a family in exchange for security, management, maintenance, and custodial care. About every ten years, minimal funds were allocated for stopgap measures. There was talk of preservation, but, good intentions aside, nothing was actually done to correct several underlying, crucial problems. Its condition deteriorated shamefully.

In the early 1930s, the Great Depression strangled the entire country, and Louisiana was no exception. Surplus funds to restore an old, worn-out building were nonexistent. However, as a result of the Depression, federal work projects were created, and one of those projects ultimately saved the Old State House.

In 1937, the Works Progress Administration, at the urging of concerned Louisianans, approved funding for a major renovation. Federal and state governments shared the $46,280 price tag. The goal was to create modern office space while retaining the architectural integrity of the structure. Eighty-six men from the WPA and nine supplied by the state administration began work on an extensive list of renovation projects in November of 1937.[1] *State Times* reporter Orene Muse wrote, "the white men and the negroes on the relief rolls have gone about the thousand-and-one tasks incident to repairing the building for use as a museum." First among those tasks was ridding the structure of bats, pigeons, and rats given free access to the building through countless broken windows.[2]

Soon after restoration began, a fire almost negated any need for the project. In the early morning hours of December 13, a night watchman discovered the blaze in the southwest wing. Someone had left a gas heater burning overnight, and it ignited nearby materials. One room was damaged, and a hole was burned in the floor of the room above it. Damage was estimated at seven hundred dollars.[3]

Years of dirt and grime were removed from every area of the building. Plaster, stucco, and cement were repaired on both interior and exterior walls. Broken light fixtures were repaired and polished. Missing fixtures, many taken by souvenir hunters or vandals, were replaced. An irate foreman recounted how an antique hunter had offered a custodian fifteen hundred dollars for one of the House chamber chandeliers. Paint was scraped from marble mantels. New plumbing was installed, electric fixtures were repaired, and missing hardware was replaced. Part of the structure holding the glass panels in the dome was rebuilt, and missing or broken stained glass was replaced with European glass at the exorbitant cost of $1.50 per square foot. Everything was freshly painted. Interior walls were painted light buff and trimmed in brown. The rotunda was trimmed in gold, and ceilings were painted ivory.[4] The exterior was painted stone gray, with silver aluminum paint on the metal window frames and black trim on the ledges.[5] Copper was placed on the sixteen different roofs, and copper gutters were hung to accommodate excess rainwater.[6] The once-beautiful grounds surrounding the Old State House were terraced and graded,[7] and the aging iron fence was repaired and painted shiny black.[8]

A small oak tree, struggling to survive, had to be removed from atop the northwest tower before the exterior could be repaired. It had grown there, its roots gripping the brick and masonry, for as long as anyone could remember. The determined roots had created large cracks as they forced themselves between the bricks in search of moisture. When the tree was removed, three hundred pounds of masonry and corroded cast iron fell from the tower. In a tribute to its tenacity, the little oak was planted near the old zoo by the railroad track in City Park.[9]

As the beloved building regained its dignity, reporter Orene Muse eloquently expressed the people's joy at seeing it restored: "And the old statehouse will begin a new era in its history. Perhaps not the fiery era of its youth, nor the splendor of its middle age, but a quiet era of old age where mellowness and quiet graces have their sway."[10]

The WPA renovation went so well that, even before it was complete, an additional fifty-five thousand dollars was sought to extend the project. Phase II, begun in June 1938, called for a modern steam-heating system, repairs to the ancient elevator, improvements to plumbing facilities, and grand plans for landscaping the grounds.[11]

The ambitious landscape plan was carried out by 125 men. The old pond, which once yielded hidden Civil War treasures and a skeleton, was filled in. Eight thousand plants were ordered from E. A. McIlhenny's Avery Island Jungle Gardens. Camellias were planted along the Front Street walk leading to the main entrance. Camellias and azaleas adorned the terraces. Formerly weed-infested grounds were seeded with St. Augustine and Bermuda grass. Climbing junipers and evergreens lined the fence of the lower grounds on North Boulevard and Front Street. Six large magnolia trees were planted on the upper west sidewalk. Groups of azaleas and camellias graced the low-lying grounds between the terrace and Front Street, and an irrigation system with nine hydrants was installed to quench the plants' thirst.

Project superintendent W. C. Martin was understandably proud of the WPA project. He made every penny count and, in doing so, he saved enough money to allow installation of edgewood pine floors on the second and third floors.[12]

When the WPA project was finished and the Old State House restored to its former magnificence, the modern offices were in great demand. The WPA headquarters remained in the building, and other federal agencies joined them. The Louisiana Art Commission, created in 1938, also opened its offices there.[13]

Phase III of the WPA project involved no cleaning or construction at all. This final project was sponsored by the Louisiana Library Commission and was completed in 1940. The Baton Rouge unit of the Louisiana Writer's Project wrote a brief history of the renovated building called *Old State Capitol, A Sketch*. It concludes with the haunting statement, "Over all broods a feeling of antiquity, as if the ghosts of the great men of Louisiana who once passed through its halls had left a trace of their greatness behind them."[14]

In the early 1940s, the country was once again at war, and nothing was spared from its effects. Patriotic citizens were asked to seek out and donate scrap metal for use in the war effort. Many in Baton Rouge, especially those with sons serving in the military, believed the fence surrounding the capitol should be offered to the government as a show of support for our troops.[15] Others were shocked at the suggestion of destroying such a beautiful, historic relic when the supply of worthless scrap metal was not yet exhausted. In a letter to the editor of the *State Times*, C. A. Ives wrote that the fence should not be torn down because it, along with the Old State House, provided a link to our forefathers and to the history of the state. Its destruction should be allowed only under the most dire circumstances.[16] Fortunately, the fence was not needed, and the controversy over its donation was moot.

World War II did have its effect on the Old State Capitol, as it was now commonly called, in that upkeep and repairs were completely neglected. However, in spite of its condition and deficiencies, the building remained occupied by numerous veterans' organizations, state commissions, and examining boards.

In 1946, the legislature appropriately dedicated the Old State Capitol as a memorial to Louisianans who had lost their lives in World War II. All the elements of a grand ceremony were present: flags, bands, speakers, pastors, veterans, and elected officials. The dedication ceremony was planned for the grounds, but rainy weather forced it inside to the House chamber.[17]

It was not until 1947, ten years after the WPA renovation, that any money was allocated for repairs. Twenty thousand dollars was spent on upkeep and reparation. As with the WPA restoration, the latest round of repairs was not intended to change the appearance of the building, merely to maintain it. Once again, walls were plastered and repainted. The electrical system, said to be the same one installed when first wired for electricity, was replaced to meet modern demands and safety standards. In addition, a water stack was installed from the basement to the top floor with outlets on each floor to reduce the risk of destruction by fire.[18]

In 1948, the legislature reaffirmed the building's dedication to veterans, but this time gave the measure some teeth. It created the Old State Capitol Memorial Commission, a five-member board of veterans charged with administration of the building, and, most importantly, it allocated five thousand dollars per year to carry out the board's mission. Members of the first commission were Fred Dent, chairman; Larry Bahan, vice chairman; Albert Isenberg, secretary; Niles P. Evans; and George W. Wilder, Jr.[19] They served without pay. For the next ten years, the Old State Capitol Commission actively tried to keep the building repaired and usable by veterans, the group it was dedicated to serve and honor, but it was almost impossible to keep up with the deterioration of a very old building in the heat and humidity of south Louisiana. In spite of its shabbiness, the building remained occupied and well used.[20]

Following World War II, well-known American radio personality and commentator Drew Pearson conceived a plan to collect food and clothing to aid the people of war-ravaged Europe whose lives had been devastated and who were left with nothing. It was called the Friendship Train. The people of France, touched by the generosity of Americans, created their own program as a thank-you. A World War I vintage train, forty-nine boxcars in all, was loaded with gifts from French people of all walks of life. The "Merci" train, or gratitude train, was of the "40 and 8" type (40 men, 8 horses) narrow-gauge track model.[21]

One boxcar was sent for each of the forty-eight states, and the forty-ninth was shared between the District of Columbia and the territory of Hawaii. The boxcar for Louisiana arrived in Baton Rouge in February 1949 and was received with such fanfare as had not been seen in many years. Gov. Earl K. Long accepted the gift from French consul general Lionel Vasse following a parade complete with floats, bands, and a flyover of military planes. The contents were displayed at the new capitol for a short time before being distributed, but in April, the boxcar itself was placed on the northeast corner of the grounds of the Old State Capitol.[22]

Drew Pearson, creator of the Friendship Train to France, delivered his radio broadcast from the boxcar on the Old State Capitol grounds the day of the official dedication ceremony on June 12, 1949. By this time, a lovely pavilion, built with locally donated materials and services, had been constructed over the train to shield it from the harsh Louisiana elements. Pearson was most complimentary of Louisiana's effort to honor both its friendship with France and the gift boxcar.[23]

About the time of the boxcar dedication, Gov. Earl Long suggested to the state board of liquidation that if any funds were left at the end of the fiscal year, they should be given to the Old State Capitol Memorial Commission. In June of 1949, the commission was granted $10,881, which were used to repair the leaky roof[24] and to provide recreational and kitchen facilities for veterans.[25] In 1950, the old elevator, installed in 1917 and condemned in 1935, was removed from the southeast corner of the rotunda.[26] A new elevator, required by aging veterans who found it difficult to climb stairs, was installed in May of 1951, much to the delight of the building's occupants. It cost $18,000.[27]

By 1953, a snack shop called The Fox Hole, a veterans' lounge, and a poolroom were located in the basement. Upstairs, the Senate chamber was used as a recreation room. The House chamber was used for meetings and art exhibits. A variety of city, state, and federal agencies occupied offices in the Old State Capitol, including the Louisiana Art Commission, Parish Civil Defense, Forestry Commission, Barber Board, and army and navy recruiting.[28]

Everything seemed to be going along smoothly until 1953, when the fire marshal's office condemned the building and threatened to close it unless numerous fire hazards were immediately corrected. Large vertical openings, notably the rotunda and the second-floor wooden stairways, created dangerous fire situations. An unprotected, gas-fired steam boiler operated in the basement, and a steel smokestack rose to the roof through one corner of the rotunda. There was no emergency lighting. An automatic sprinkler system was the recommended, but costly, solution. Although administered by the Old State Capitol Memorial Commission, the building was maintained by the state Division of Building and Grounds, which had recently incurred unusual expenses on the new state capitol. As usual, funds were not available for state-of-the-art equipment. Even though many agencies occupied offices, only one—the Barber Board—paid rent, and that was only a paltry thirty-six dollars per month. Until the best fire-preventation measures could be installed, it was agreed that a fire standpipe with a pump to provide adequate water pressure and hoses on each floor would allow the building to remain open.[29] The hoses were installed, but two years later, a reporter said they did little to calm the fears of those who loved the building and realized the preventative measures taken would be ineffective against a major fire.[30]

Finally, in 1955, almost twenty years after the WPA renovation, and at the urging of the D.A.R. and other historic preservation groups, the Old State Capitol Memorial Commission made a bold move. It authorized an engineer to thoroughly survey the building to assess its needs. The commission then went to the legislature with a detailed list of the building's requirements and a realistic cost estimate—approximately a quarter of a million dollars.[31] The well-planned presentation commanded the attention of the legislature, and two separate appropriation bills were filed, one for $269,900, the other for $350,000. A *State Times* reporter wrote about the building's shameful condition. He found huge chunks of fallen plaster, both inside and out. Electric fixtures dangled from the walls, exposing frayed wiring. The electrical system, which "might have been the envy of Thomas Edison when he saw the first glimmer of light in that incandescent bulb," was completely incapable of meeting increased technological demands. Every door, floor, and wall needed repairing, patching, or replacing. The roof leaked, and a sprinkler system was needed. It seemed that only the pigeons, spiders, and other creatures inhabiting the building were comfortable in their surroundings.[32]

In a great stroke of luck—possibly the only luck the building ever had—the legislature approved the $350,000 appropriation; in fact, it gave even more than the commission asked for. The extra funds were given to ensure the work would be done under contract to the state and awarded by bids. As with past rehabilitations, this project was not intended to change the Old State Capitol in any drastic way, but simply to keep it standing and usable.[33]

Renovations were completed in November of 1956. Jay Broussard, a member of the Old State Capitol Memorial Commission, said that the only obvious changes were "the removal and storage of old lighting fixtures until funds [were] obtained to restore them, leveling of the floor in the old Senate chamber, widening of some staircases and installation of fire doors." The exterior was painted beige-gray with green and light-gray trim. The rotunda was painted peach with light-blue trim. The House chamber on the second floor was used as an art gallery, so high ceilings were lowered to eight feet with "egg crate" panels, and pegboards were placed on the walls to display art. Windows, floors, and cracks in walls were repaired. Part of the basement was painted, tidied, and air conditioned for use as a war museum.[34]

An open house was held in January 1957 to reopen the structure after the renovation. Visitors marveled at the bright fluorescent lighting throughout the building, the new roof, the new $150,000 sprinkler system, and the $50,000 electrical system. The beautiful Senate chamber was turned into a ballroom for nonprofit organizations. The Old State Capitol once again came to life, and all of its offices were occupied.[35]

Chapter Ten

Fight for Identity and Resurrection

The Old State Capitol enjoyed a period of renewed energy following its latest renovation, but the building and fence were in constant need of repair. Ten years later, another major restoration began. Baton Rouge, which residents say always had a "small town" atmosphere, began to grow. On occasion, that growth resulted in attention focused on the old building. With attention came money, and with money came renewed controversy over who should manage the building. Those feuds once again pitted Baton Rouge against New Orleans and were some of the bitterest battles yet.

In 1961, Front Street was widened. Front Street, called Natchez Street when the Old State Capitol was built and now known as River Road, was the western boundary of the grounds. To accommodate the wider road, the fence along the western edge of the property was removed and carefully rebuilt sixteen feet closer to the building. It was the first time the perimeter of the grounds had been altered in any way.[1]

On September 10, 1965, Hurricane Betsy roared through Louisiana. Although substantially inland, Baton Rouge and the Old State House were no match for Betsy's high winds and torrential rain. Strong gusts blew out many of the windows in and above the dome. Plunging glass shattered on the marble floor as debris and water poured into the rotunda.[2]

In November, the Committee for Preservation of Historical Monuments asked the Louisiana Capitol Construction and Improvements Commission for a half-million dollars to restore the damaged building.[3] The commission did not approve enough for an extensive restoration, but okayed $250,000 to repair damage done to the dome by Hurricane Betsy as well as to the water-soaked interior walls and floors. The broken stained-glass panes were replaced with genuine glass instead of the suggested sturdier plastic. In addition, the rotunda and balconies were to be redone, exterior walls waterproofed, and a new roof installed. George M. Leake of New Orleans was named architect for the project.[4] Less than a month later the same commission approved $429,376 in additional funds for the restoration.[5]

By early 1968, the scope of the project and the allocation of funds had increased once again. Architect Leake and contractor Milton Womack of Baton Rouge directed the most extensive restoration since the WPA project. This time, the renovation was geared toward restoring the building to its original historical identity instead of trying to divide it into small office spaces. The cost was estimated at $672,000 and required undoing much of the work accomplished during previous modernizations and restorations.[6] Lowered ceilings and partitions used to create offices on each side of the Senate and House chambers were removed. Other large rooms that had been carved into smaller offices were also restored to their original sizes. Vending machines were removed from the rotunda. Central heating and air conditioning were installed. The walls that had been placed behind the ironwork in the corners of the second-floor gallery to provide restroom space were removed. The interior was painted "hospital green," and the exterior was waterproofed and painted.[7] Lamps at the base of the stairs and others on the first floor were removed, to be replaced with restored originals or reproductions. However, almost ten years later, the lamps were still not installed. Leake explained that they were in such an awful state of disrepair that he had spent several years looking for a company that would even attempt a restoration before finding one in New York. He said the missing lamps would be installed within a month.[8]

About midway through the restoration, the newly painted exterior walls caused quite a stir—the building was a bright mustard yellow. The public was quickly assured that the yellow was only zinc oxide, a primer for the top coat. The final color was beige with light and dark brown trim.[9]

Less than a year later, the seemingly never-ending problem of water leakage during heavy rains resurfaced. The freshly painted interior walls became water stained, and soggy ceiling tiles on the first floor collapsed. Wastebaskets, carefully placed to catch dripping water, dotted office floors. The contractor attributed the problem to cracked slate on the roof and a missing hatch on one of the flat roofs. He vowed to fix the problem immediately.[10]

Funds to repair or restore the building were always scarce and, as such, were always used on the building itself. The iron fence surrounding the grounds received only an occasional coat of paint. More than 110 years after its construction, it was corroded and dangerous. In 1971, an appropriation of ten thousand dollars was sought for repairs, but the request was denied.[11] A year later, the Louisiana Board of Liquidation of the State Debt gave most of the funds needed for the project, and the Baton Rouge City-Parish Council supplied the rest. Pearce Foundry, Inc. of Prairieville cast molds to create new sections of the fence.[12] Massive oleander plants growing through and over the fence were removed, as they were damaging the fence and hiding the building from view.[13]

In the early 1970s, the fence was seriously threatened. City planners in Baton Rouge began to discuss building a civic center just to the south of the Old State Capitol. Some wanted to remove the southern fence to create one large public area with walkways connecting the civic center's newly landscaped grounds and fountains with the historic, terraced grounds of the Old State Capitol. The proposal raised the ire of preservationists opposed to any change in the design or placement of the fence. Three ladies, Mrs. J. A. Tucker, Mrs. Irving Dameron, and Mrs. P. Chauvin Wilkinson, with the help of Mrs. Ruth LeCompte, researched, gathered information, and in almost record time nominated the Old State Capitol to the National Register of Historic Places. The nomination was approved in January 1973, placing it among the nation's most historically and architecturally significant properties. There was a twofold benefit from the designation. It meant the building would be eligible for federal matching funds for restoration.[14] More importantly to the preservationists, it also meant that changing anything about the state-owned land would be a much more difficult process requiring research and several layers of approval.[15] Ultimately, the determined ladies had their way. The southern fence today remains almost exactly as it was when erected in the late 1850s, without so much as a connecting gate to the civic center.

During construction of the civic center, cracks began to appear in both interior and exterior walls of the Old State Capitol. Some feared they were the result of excavation and pile driving at the nearby construction site. The cracks, which were measured and monitored closely, sometimes appeared and sometimes closed up without explanation, suggesting the building was shifting. Construction continued, but no permanent damage was noted in the former capitol.[16]

Mrs. Tucker, Mrs. Wilkinson, and Mrs. Dameron also spearheaded an effort to nominate the building for the nation's highest historical honor. In 1976, the Old State Capitol was named a National Historic Landmark, meaning it "has significance for all Americans in commemorating the nation's past."[17] The group formed The Committee on the Governor's Room with the goal of restoring the governor's office and adjoining reception room as "a means of interpreting the history of the building to visitors." The committee of seven held its first meeting in June of 1976. Ruth LeCompte was chairman. Six months later, Sandra Thompson, secretary of the Department of Culture, Recreation and Tourism, appointed a committee to oversee long-range plans and guidelines for displays in the building. The Governor's Room Committee became the Old State Capitol Committee. Mrs. Howard Samuel was named overall coordinator, and members of the CRT staff served in an advisory capacity. Their statement of intent read in part, "The purpose of this committee is to insure that the Old State Capitol because of its unique architecture, its association with historic events and its affectionate place in the hearts of Louisianans be restored, maintained and utilized in a manner compatible with its National Landmark status."[18]

In 1978, management of the building was placed in the

Department of Parks (a division of the Department of Culture, Recreation and Tourism). The name of the oversight committee changed to the Old State Capitol Executive Committee, then to the Old State Capitol Advisory Committee.[19]

During this time, underscoring the need for security and permanent management, a bust of former governor Francis T. Nicholls was stolen from the rotunda during a social event.[20] An anonymous caller, feeling pangs of conscience, informed the police the sculpture could be found in a paper bag at a specific location. It was, and Nicholls was returned to his proper place in the rotunda.[21]

In 1979, reflecting the persistence of preservationists, the legislature passed a Historic Preservation Act and appropriated funds for an extensive restoration. A master plan for restoration was accepted from architect John Desmond. It recommended "restoration of the first and second floors to the same condition as when it was used as the state capitol." Offices would be relegated to the ground, third, and fourth floors. Social events would no longer be allowed.[22] Seeking funds to begin restoration of the seriously deteriorating building, the Old State Capitol Advisory Committee approached the East Baton Rouge legislative delegation and asked it to press for inclusion in the capital outlay bill of 1980.[23] Their efforts were rewarded with an appropriation of $250,000 for the architectural planning phase of restoration. That's when things began to get sticky, and local columnist Anne Price declared the building "Mired in Political Ooze." Governmental bureaucracy had placed the building under the jurisdiction of at least three different state agencies. When the time came to select an architect for the project, the Architect Selection Board could not reach a decision from among the forty-one proposals submitted.[24] More than a year later, a New Orleans firm, E. Eean McNaughton and Associates, was chosen from among the twenty-four architectural firms submitting second-round proposals.[25]

Before any work began, Gov. David Treen announced the allocation of $2.5 million for restoration of the Old State Capitol and placement of the building in the Louisiana State Museum system.[26] Preservationists welcomed the seemingly appropriate, single-agency oversight. The state museum system oversaw ten properties, eight of them in New Orleans, one in Shreveport, and one in Baton Rouge. Most museum board members lived in New Orleans. The law transferring the Old State Capitol to the museum system also required a local support group, which museum director Robert Macdonald welcomed as a way to increase local interest. The Old State Capitol Committee, already in place and active for years, became the Old State Capitol Associates, the official support group for the Old State Capitol.[27]

The first task for architect Eean McNaughton, who served as the lead architect on the project, was to create a historic structures report, deemed critical for any serious restoration. It would document, as accurately as possible, the original appearance of the Old State Capitol. Architectural plans for restoration could not begin until the report was complete, because no one knew just how much could be accomplished with the funds available. The report required months of research to determine every historical, structural, and aesthetic detail of the building. The Old State Capitol Associates were especially interested in the report's recommendation to use the building as a museum. Work was expected to begin sometime in 1984 and to continue for several years.[28] It seemed that the Old State House would finally receive the attention it desperately needed and be restored to its former glory.

The eagerly awaited report determining the future of the Old State Capitol was revealed in November 1983. The Associates and local supporters were completely stunned by the recommendation that the dignified old governmental building house a museum of Louisiana folklife. The governor's suite would contain exhibits on the history of the building, but the remainder of the exhibits would focus on the folk cultures of Louisiana. A café or restaurant was planned for the first floor, along with a museum store featuring folk art.[29] As recorded by Joan Samuel, president of the Associates, "The long awaited master plan was presented—and much to the chagrin of many OSCA members—called for the building to become the center for Louisiana Folklife." Critics thought the folklife concept was neither appropriate for nor compatible with the history of the building.[30]

For months, tension mounted and tempers flared as Baton Rouge supporters of the Old State Capitol dismissed the idea as demeaning and suggested that New Orleans wanted to dump its folk collection on Baton Rouge. The local Associates organization favored a plan that would make the Old State Capitol a museum of historical and political exhibits, which they saw as more representative of the character and architecture of the building. Robert Macdonald, state museum director, was dismayed by the strenuous objections to a folklife museum. He believed a museum of political history would be "static."[31] Local preservationist Mrs. Stuart Johnson responded, "We do not agree that an historical museum is a dead museum. . . . Heaven knows, Louisiana provides the excitement for it."[32]

Eventually a compromise was reached, allowing a large portion of the first floor to house political and historical exhibits. The storm temporarily subsided as all involved were anxious to begin the restoration. The building closed in early 1985, and a groundbreaking ceremony was held in May. Phase I, funded by the legislature with $2.5 million, included stabilizing the structure, repairing exterior walls and windows, refurbishing the stained-glass dome, and replacing the roof with one of solid copper.[33]

Robert Reilly, curator of the Old State Capitol, documented progress on the construction in notes to the Associates organization in 1986. He wrote of scaffolding built on the second floor reaching the top of the dome. Each of the 2,054 pieces of colored glass in the dome was carefully removed, catalogued, cleaned, and stored while the wooden structure holding them was repaired. Each pane was then returned to its original place.[34] A wooden catwalk in the lantern above the dome was replaced with a steel grate, allowing more light to illuminate the stained glass.[35] Workmen discovered a serious structural problem in the House chamber—two major support beams, forty-one and sixty-one feet in length, sagged. They were leveled and supported with bolted steel plates, a remarkable architectural/engineering feat.[36] While repairing the beams, workmen discovered asbestos in the building. By August of

1986, most construction was complete, but the building remained closed due in part to the asbestos. In another stroke of bad luck, state budget problems forced cuts in staff for all state-run museums, forcing them to reduce hours and days of operation. No one knew when the building would once again open to the public.

The uncertainty was tremendously frustrating to Baton Rougeans, who desperately wanted the cherished building and premiere tourist attraction open even if it meant being staffed by volunteers. James Sefcik, new director of the state museum system, believed the building should remain closed until exhibits were in place. He changed his mind upon visiting Baton Rouge and seeing that the building itself was a magnificent exhibit. He was optimistic about reopening quickly.[37]

More than three years after the capitol closed for restoration, through the efforts of Baton Rouge civic leaders anxious to revitalize the downtown area and tourism, it was announced that the Old State Capitol would reopen on July 4, 1988. It was still only partially renovated as interior restoration had not been included in Phase I. Sixty thousand dollars left over from the restoration was used to give a quick face-lift to the rotunda and the fence.[38] Paint had chipped off walls, and one ceiling had collapsed because the building had been closed without air-conditioning or humidity control for over a year. Neutral gray interior paint was touched up, and the fence was painted sage green. Light fixtures replicated from drawings and photographs were placed around the rail of the second-floor rotunda. A few modest exhibits, mostly panel-board stands, were placed in some of the rooms. The House and Senate chambers were not air-conditioned and could be seen only by peering through plexiglass barriers. The fire marshal limited access to the second floor to fifty visitors, because there were no enclosed stairways.[39] Phase II of the master plan was still in the future, but for now, Baton Rougeans were elated at having the Old State Capitol back on even a limited basis.

Soon after the reopening the legislature approved $450,000 to build interior stairways, required by fire regulations to allow greater access to the second floor. The project was delayed to determine which of the two offices adjoining the governor's reception office had been the actual working office of governors who served in the State House. Only in late 1989 did museum officials discover the exact location of Governor Long's office. A former legislator, Ragan D. Madden, was a wealth of information and distinctly remembered the office. He recalled seeking a job from family friend and then-governor Huey Long. Long hired Madden to run the elevator after he fired the woman who had been running it but who had not voted for him. Madden also remembered helping move to the new state capitol and finding a large sum of Confederate money in the basement. It was thought to have no value, so it was burned.[40]

During the time when historians were trying to determine which room was the actual governor's office and where they should build the stairs, the premiere property of the State Museum System, the Cabildo in New Orleans, was severely damaged by fire. Because the state funds appropriated for stairs at the Old State Capitol were not yet being used to build stairs, the commissioner of administration, Dennis Stine, suggested diverting the money for use at the Cabildo.[41] The move infuriated Baton Rougeans, who believed it was a step toward closing the Old State Capitol, and served as fuel for the simmering argument that the New Orleans-based museum board cared little for its properties outside of their own city. The museum board argued that, because the second floor of the Old State Capitol was not air-conditioned, it would serve no purpose to allow increased visitation on that floor.[42] In June, a legislative committee voted to keep the funds for use at the Old State Capitol. The Baton Rouge city-parish government, understanding the importance of the unique landmark to the city, offered to let the state tie into the heating and cooling system of the city civic-center complex, addressing the serious problem of climate control in the Old State Capitol museum.[43]

In 1989, the Old State Capitol Associates engaged Mary Louise Prudhomme to organize a large event in the building designed to attract the attention of legislators. Preservationist Elise Rosenthal; president of the Senate Allen Bares; his executive assistant, Sylvia Duke; commissioner of administration Brian Kendrick; Senate secretary Mike Baer; and Prudhomme devised a plan to host the opening of the 1990 legislature in the former State Capitol. Supporters hoped the ceremony would make legislators, many of whom had never been in the building, aware of the importance of the structure and more willing to support its restoration.[44]

Tom Ed McHugh, soft-spoken mayor-president of Baton Rouge, was unwittingly drawn into a brewing storm when he scheduled a luncheon in the governors' office. He believed he had permission to use the Old State Capitol for the event and even went so far as to write a thank-you note to James Sefcik. According to the *State Times,* on the day of the meeting, Sefcik and three state museum board members came to Baton Rouge and tried to stop the meeting. Sefcik told the mayor, "This is an illegal meeting. You are in my building." McHugh supposedly replied, "You are in my city." Later, McHugh said things had been blown out of proportion.[45]

April was a month of great turmoil. The dream of interior renovation was just within reach because almost six million dollars was in the capital outlay bill to fund Phase II of the restoration,[46] but the arguments between Baton Rouge interests and the state museum board were escalating. Suddenly, an unexpected new proposal was thrown into the ring. The Baton Rouge legislative delegation, led by Rep. Raymond Jetson, suggested that a local nine-person commission take control of the old building. Jetson believed it could be a fine political museum, but it had been treated as an unwanted "stepchild" by the New Orleans-based State Museum Board.[47] Members of that board replied that they had been diligent in caring for the structure and believed a local board would result in a "lack of professionalism."[48]

In the midst of the controversy and uncertainty, plans progressed for the opening of the legislature. The event required complicated arrangements for the building, which had not held a legislative opening since 1932. It was discovered that termites infested the building and the sprinkler system had been turned off.[49] When state officials gathered at the somewhat shabby Old State Capitol on Monday, April 16, a city fire truck stood nearby with its ladder extended to a second-floor window to act as a fire escape in case of emergency. Air-conditioning was pumped in. Before the impressive ceremony, legislators gathered on the steps overlooking the terraced grounds and sang "You Are My Sunshine" as they waited for photographers to snap a group photograph. Bands played and jets roared overhead. Senators and representatives adjourned to their respective chambers before convening jointly in the House chamber to hear Gov. Buddy Roemer's address. Soldiers in period uniforms added historic flavor. Lunch was served in rooms decorated with melting ice sculptures before legislators returned to the new capitol to conduct the state's business.[50]

The calculated move paid off. Legislators were almost unanimous in their support of restoring the beautiful building, but the fight for control put the funds in jeopardy. Feelings of sectional rivalry, first described in 1850 and never buried very deeply, resurfaced. Almost all New Orleans-area legislators favored leaving the State Museum Board in control, while most of the rest favored some sort of local control but were hesitant to create another layer of bureaucracy.[51]

Faced with considerable opposition to his bill, Jetson approached Secretary of State Fox McKeithen. McKeithen agreed to place the building and museum in the archives division of the Office of the Secretary of State. Jetson amended his bill to place control of the building in the already existing agency, hoping to increase its chance of passing.[52] He said,

> While we appreciate the importance of such pretty children as the Presbytere and the U.S. Mint, we in Baton Rouge are serving notice that our prize, our jewel in the crown, the Old State Capitol, will no longer be treated as a stepchild who is thrown the rotting crusts of decaying appropriations.

James Sefcik, chair of the museum board, countered that they had sought appropriation from the legislature for many years but had always been turned down.[53] The editors of the *Baton Rouge Morning Advocate* expressed regret that the matter had become "a contest between New Orleans and Baton Rouge."[54] In May, the hostility escalated even more as New Orleans senator Dennis

Bagneris, Jr. filed a bill to remove the Division of Archives, Records Management and History from the Secretary of State's Office and to place it in the State Museum System of the Department of Culture, Recreation and Tourism. However, such a move would have required a change in the constitution.[55]

When Jetson's bill came before the proper House committee, New Orleans representative Arthur Morrell pounded the gavel and tried to adjourn the meeting. When that failed, he proposed an amendment limiting funds for the Old State Capitol and imposing unique restrictions on it, but that also failed. After much political wrangling and shouting, the committee voted eight to six to send the motion to the full House.[56] The House also passed the bill but amended it to require an appointed fifteen-member advisory board of people from across the state.[57] The House bill placing the Old State Capitol under the auspices of the Secretary of State sailed through a Senate committee and passed the full Senate by a vote of twenty-three to fifteen despite the pleas of Sen. Jon Johnson of New Orleans, who begged the Senate not to put the building "in the hands of a bunch of neophytes . . . who really and truly don't know what they're doing."[58] The legislation was signed into law by Gov. Buddy Roemer.

In June of 1991, the Old State Capitol once again closed, but this time the closing was met with celebration because Phase II, restoration of the interior, was about to begin. A ceremony on the grounds allowed the public to bid farewell to the beloved building. The air was filled with the sound of music and the aroma of food. Crowds cheered when Union soldiers surrendered to Confederate troops in a Civil War re-enactment. Candidates for governor delivered old-fashioned stump speeches, and guests took a last glimpse at the soon-to-be-closed building.[59] Two days later, dignitaries officially closed the Old State Capitol in a ceremony that included a delegation from the St. James Lodge (Masons), the same organization that had participated in the cornerstone ceremony in 1847.[60]

Before restoration work could begin, the Old State Capitol had to be stripped of all the trappings of modernity. Old, lowered, acoustic-tile ceilings, flocked wallpaper, exposed pipes and insulation, carpeted floors, makeshift restrooms, office partitions, and much more had to be removed from every hall and room of the building. Workers stripped away years of grime and tons of inaccurate materials, and the toxic asbestos discovered in floors and walls during Phase I of the restoration required lengthy and costly removal. Bids were let in December and work began in March 1992.[61]

As layer after layer of previous renovations were removed, the old building revealed secrets hidden for over a century. Workmen discovered areas of charred and smoke-stained wood and brick dating from the fire of 1862, when Union troops occupied the building. Other discoveries gave rare glimpses into the building's pre-Civil War interior. After removing restrooms from the east wall of the House chamber, they found evidence of two doors on either side of the main door leading into the second-floor rotunda. They were arched, the same height as the center door, and about five feet wide.[62] They also found evidence of an arched door on the rear (east) wall of the House chamber leading to a gallery on the third floor.[63] (The third-floor gallery was not rebuilt in Freret's 1882 restoration.)

A lovely curved ceiling under the arch in the Senate chamber was removed, allowing the full height and beauty of the stained-glass window to glow once again inside the room. The ceiling, installed after the fire of 1906, hid over half of the window and covered the charred frame. The topmost portion of the window was left charred and uncovered as a graphic reminder of that fire. The ceiling also hid small round windows, similar to those on the north and south walls, facing into the towers.[64]

Old graffiti, some dating back to the 1880s, covered the walls of one small room high in the southern tower of the House chamber. The barely accessible room now contains mechanical equipment but was previously a hideaway for legislative pages, many of whom signed the walls. The signatures, dates, and sentiments remain untouched.

Almost no evidence existed indicating the appearance of the interior in Dakin's 1850 building, but a substantial amount of evidence remained as to what the building looked like following Freret's restoration in 1882. All involved agreed it should be restored to the latter period. The Senate chamber was restored to the period of 1906, the time following the destructive fire in that room.[65]

Every aspect of construction received detailed attention. Crown molding was hand-drawn and made on-site with tools crafted using age-old techniques. Freret had chosen hinges and door handles from the P. F. Corbin Company catalogue and recorded their numbers in his specifications, so the magnificent bronze hardware was carefully re-created from the catalogue's illustrations.[66] The state seal was added to door handles, and brass chandeliers re-created from old photographs were hung in each legislative chamber.[67]

A team of craftsmen from New York applied gold leaf to over four hundred rosettes in the House and Senate chambers. Gold leaf was also applied to the main support beam and other details in the rotunda, as well as on the ceiling and columns in the House chamber. The same company used artisans from around the world to paint unfinished cypress to resemble oak, a labor-intensive technique called faux bois.[68] Specifications for the pine floors called for a minimum of ten grain lines per inch. Such a high standard yields floors that are amazingly strong and durable.[69] The House chamber was also wired for television and is now capable of holding major production events.[70]

In the fall of 1993, construction began to wind down. Secretary of State Fox McKeithen, the contractor, and craftsmen signed the back of the final piece of crown molding before placing it on the wall of the treasurer's office.[71]

Focus began to shift from construction to the exhibits and grounds. The National Archives agreed to loan the original Louisiana Purchase documents if display conditions were satisfactory. A case with special wood, bulletproof glass, temperature controls, and fiber-optic lighting was built to showcase the document,[72] which was on display for six months. An exhibit in the old governor's office transported the viewer back into history with a podium and two teleprompters. At the touch of a button, the teleprompters showed videos of colorful political figures in action as transcripts of their speeches scrolled by.

On May 1, 1994, the Old State Capitol opened in resplendent glory as the Center for Political and Governmental History of Louisiana and was once again dedicated to Louisiana's veterans. Activities, music, and crafts filled the grounds. A fireworks display capped the day's festivities. Among the many guests were people who had worked in the building long ago. They recalled earlier times and rejoiced at its current beauty.[73]

Since the rebirth of the Old State Capitol as a political museum, the building has been well used for a variety of political and social events. On January 8, 1996, Murphy J. "Mike" Foster was sworn in as governor on the grounds of the Old State Capitol—the first inauguration since that of Huey Pierce Long in 1932. Foster, who was "overwhelmed with a sense of history," chose the site because his grandfather, Murphy J. Foster, had been sworn in as governor on the same grounds exactly one hundred years earlier. Platforms and stands were built on the terraces of the west grounds. Spectators braved the bitter cold to see the inauguration, hear brief speeches, and enjoy patriotic music, a jet flyover, and a cannon salute. History had indeed repeated itself.[74]

In 2004, Phase III, a two-year, $7.6 million restoration of the exterior, began. The building is made of old brick, in some places three feet thick, covered with plaster, and scored to resemble stone. Through the years as the plaster and brickwork crumbled, modern fixes—mostly concrete—were applied. In hindsight, the well-intentioned repairs were probably detrimental to the building. Relatively hard, modern building materials applied over soft, more porous materials allowed moisture to become trapped in the walls, quickening deterioration. The building was stripped of all plaster, revealing the original bricks for which James Dakin had fought and been arrested. Restoration architect Jerry Campbell arranged for a specialist in historic materials to teach workers the proper mixture, consistency, and application of a "breathable" plaster to cover the old brick. All exterior windows were removed, restored, and reseated. Iron surrounding each window, as well as other decorative iron trimming, was stripped and refinished. Every pane of the huge stained-glass windows in each legislative chamber was removed, cleaned, and replaced. The building was painted a natty off-white with ecru trim. Campbell said, "This building is dear to the heart of everybody in Louisiana. We're making sure it lasts another 300 years."[75]

Two important aspects of the Old State Capitol complex remain to be restored. One is the historically significant fence. Beginning in 2007, sections of cast iron have been removed, repaired, and replaced. The process will be repeated until all sections have been repaired. The surrounding landscape, which was largely destroyed by scaffolding during the exterior renovation, also has yet to be fully restored. A master plan to restore the grounds is being developed by the Old State Capitol staff and specialists in historic landscape.

The office of Lt. Gov. Mitch Landrieu (New Orleans) commissioned a study of all of Louisiana's museums. In August of 2005, the results were released. A consultant suggested possible consolidation of all state-owned museums into one office, whether it be the Department of Culture, Recreation and Tourism (including the State Museum system), the Secretary of State's Office, or some other entity.[76] Before any discussion of that matter could begin, hurricanes Katrina and Rita plowed into Louisiana, in August and September 2005, putting the matter to rest for the present.

Even now, the old building is revealing hidden secrets. In December of 2005, restoration workers found a deep brick-lined hole on the grounds when a wheel from a piece of heavy equipment became stuck in it. As yet, historians have not had a chance to study the hole, which is located about halfway between the Allen monument and the Old State Capitol on the upper terrace. Some believe it may be the fabled escape tunnel of Huey Long, but others believe it is more likely a vent from the basement, a relic of the old heating system. Just like a true Southern lady, the Old State Capitol will reveal its secrets slowly for years to come.

The Castellated Gothic State House is a national treasure, and thousands of tourists from every state and countless foreign countries visit every year to learn more about the unique state of Louisiana and the magnificent castle, which has presided over much of its history. Though located in Baton Rouge and dearly loved by its people, the Old State Capitol belongs to the entire state. It holds a special place in the hearts of thousands of Louisianans who have rolled down its hills, danced in its chambers, and felt proud ownership of the castle. Legislators, advisory board members from throughout the state, and the Secretary of State's staff care for it and ensure that it will indeed stand guard over the Mississippi River, Louisiana, and Baton Rouge for many future generations.

At long last the abused Old State Capitol, with its stories of survival and sorrow, politics and passion, statesmen and scoundrels, diplomacy and duplicity, has received the attention it's due and has regained the dignity worthy of its history. As one reporter so appropriately wrote decades ago,

> The sentiment about the old statehouse is only natural. And as long as its windows gleam gold when the sun sinks into the Father of Waters, so will the old building, with its quaint architecture and its memories of a distant past be treasured by Baton Rouge, by all Louisiana, and by those who journey here from afar.[77]

Appendix I

Cast Iron Lace—
The Surrounding Fence

The beautiful fence framing the Old State Capitol grounds has a history almost as deep and as troubled as the capitol itself. It was built a few years after the structure's completion and has shared some of the ups and downs of the old building. Most authorities believe James Dakin designed the fence even though he died two years before its construction began in 1854. According to Arthur Scully, Jr. in *James Dakin, Architect: His Career in New York and the South*, the original State House commissioners thought to enclose the grounds with an iron fence in 1852. They were still working closely with Dakin on finishing touches to the building and were reported to have several plans for a fence in hand. Although there is no written record of Dakin's involvement, no one argues that the design of the fence, which closely mirrors the design of the State House itself, must have been at least partially created by him.[1]

Dakin had contracted with a Pennsylvania firm for ironwork on (or inside) the State House. No record remains of who actually cast the beautiful fence, but many believe it was John Hill, owner of a Baton Rouge foundry located on Front Street (River Road) between North Street and the Pentagon Barracks. At least partial credit for the fence's design is given Hill, whose daughter reportedly had a sketch he made of the fleur-de-lis design.[2] However, a short article in *The Daily Advocate* from the period states that the fence was being cast in Baltimore and would arrive in Baton Rouge when the base was ready for it.[3]

The State House square was originally surrounded by a picket fence. In 1854, the legislature appropriated $21,630.24 to landscape the grounds, grade the lawn, provide suitable walkways, and build an iron fence meeting detailed specifications.[4] The advertisement calling for design submissions offered $250 for the accepted proposal.[5]

By late 1854, the contract had been awarded, but no construction was evident. Locals became uneasy about the lack of progress. The *Weekly Comet* expressed fears that if construction did not begin quickly, legislators might find other uses for the money in the approaching legislative session.[6] Their prodding must have spurred action, because by the next January, the foundation was in place and heavy iron sections were being set on the base.[7] Work was completed in 1855.

The delicate laciness of the fence belies its strength—it is made of cast iron. It was in its day, and still is today, an engineering marvel. The only bolts used to keep it upright are those that connect it to the base. The remainder of the sections fit together like pieces of a jigsaw puzzle. The weight of each piece supports the others. Originally built to provide security, the fence stands over seven feet tall. It completely surrounds the State House grounds and is roughly 1,575 feet long, about one third of a mile.[8] There are four gates, one each on the east and north sides, and two on the west side. Though the gates appear to swing open, the weight of each is so great that they are on supporting rollers.

The tall, iron fence is rich with symbolism. Each ten-foot section consists of several interlocking pieces, which attach to the supporting columns and rest upon one another. Sixteen cutout quatrefoils grace each wide, ornate bottom section. Each base is topped by sections of fifteen small, vertical slats. Sitting atop the small posts is a border decorated with cutout trefoils. It is important to note that the trefoils and quatrefoils are almost identical to those found in the State House, particularly those on the round windows and on the iron stairs, lending credence to the belief that the fence was Dakin's design. Each section is crowned with eight fleurs-de-lis representing Louisiana's French heritage. Each section is also nestled between large posts, and each post is topped with a pineapple, the symbol of welcome and hospitality. Some people see the pineapples as stylized magnolia pods representing the massive magnolia grandiflora trees found on the grounds for centuries.

At the center of each gate is a Roman fasces topped with a tomahawk signifying strength and unity. Instead of the fleur-de-lis, the uppermost bands of the gates are topped with stylized plants resembling sugarcane or corn. Grand eagles with outspread wings stand guard on top of the iron posts flanking each gate. The majestic birds represent liberty.[9]

The fence was spared the effects of the disastrous fire of 1862, which destroyed the interior of the State House. During Reconstruction, while the capital was in New Orleans, the fence stood guard over the ruins and the unkempt grounds. When the capitol was rebuilt following the Civil War, the fence remained intact.

It was not until 1899, when new walkways were being set around the State House grounds, that dissatisfaction with the fence surfaced. The *Daily Advocate* called for the fence to be "modernized." It suggested the fence be reduced to a height of two feet because, by city ordinance, wandering livestock was no longer a threat to the grounds or legislators.[10] Later, an anonymous citizen suggested removing the fence altogether. He called it "cumbersome" and believed it should be sold and the proceeds used to beautify the grounds.[11]

Just a few weeks after the Senate chamber fire in 1906, a large pecan tree to the right of the eastern entrance fell during a windstorm. Although that tree did not damage the fence, it caused a domino effect when it hit a magnolia tree, which fell into two other magnolias. Branches fell onto the fence, damaging it in several places.[12]

In 1910, a local newspaper once again suggested removing the fence. When unsightly wires, cables, and telephone poles were being removed from the grounds, the *Daily State-Times* said removing the fence was the last step to beautification.[13]

Fortunately, the fence was not removed, and in the 1937 Works Progress Administration restoration, it did receive a measure of much-needed attention when welders repaired cracks in the deteriorating metal.[14] The WPA project brought about the first major breach of the fence. A gate was added on the east side to accommodate entry to a new parking lot on the southeast grounds.[15] It was made in the same style and material as the original gates. The whole fence was painted an imposing "shiny black."[16]

During WWII, the fence almost fell prey to patriotic fervor. The country was asked to conserve metal and donate scrap iron to be recycled for use by United States armed forces. Some in Baton Rouge believed the fence should be donated to the campaign. Others believed the request did not include items with historic significance, and the fence should remain unless the situation became desperate. Letters to the editor came in on both sides, but ultimately, the fence was not needed as scrap iron and was once again spared from destruction.[17]

The cast iron fence and State House grounds remained virtually the same for more than one hundred years, but as Baton Rouge grew, so did traffic. To accommodate the extra volume, Front Street (formerly Natchez Street and now River Road) was widened. The entire western side of the fence was removed and rebuilt sixteen feet closer to the building. The project engineer took great pains to maintain the integrity of the fence by ensuring that each section was erected exactly as it had been.[18] At some point, the west gate (River Road) was moved. Early photographs show the west gates centered on the fence, which placed it many yards out of line with the front walk, stairs, and door. Later photographs show the gate aligned with the walkway leading to the front door of the capitol.

By the early 1970s, the fence was deteriorating badly, the old iron was becoming brittle, and missing sections were creating a safety hazard. Estimates for repairs were forty to fifty thousand dollars, but the legislature denied the funds as there was no money in the state budget for an aging fence.[19] In 1972, the legislature did appropriate ten thousand dollars for emergency repairs, augmented by $1,151 from the Baton Rouge City-Parish Council. Huge oleanders, unchecked for years, pushed on the fence as they grew over and through the iron sections. They were removed when the fence was repaired.[20] Pearce Foundry in Prairieville, Louisiana, created new molds to recast some of the fence's missing sections.[21] In a dusty corner of Pearce Foundry those molds can still be found, hidden and almost forgotten. Some, such as the eagle and pineapple (or magnolia pod), are recent, probably from the repairs of the 1970s. Others, among them the wide base, are extremely old, possibly originals passed down from the Hill Foundry following early castings or repairs.

About that time, civic leaders of Baton Rouge began to discuss a new civic center for the city. Construction on the center was planned for the area just south of the Old State Capitol. Its planners envisioned one big, public park with walkways connecting the old and new buildings. It was a nice idea, but it stirred up a hornet's nest because it required new gates at the least, and possibly even complete removal of the southern fence. Preservationists quickly set about having the building and the fence listed on the National Register of Historic Places. The coveted distinction was awarded in early 1973, and the fence was not touched.[22]

In 1982, a 150-year-old magnolia tree broke part of the southern fence. Ann Jones with the state Division of Historic Preservation, whose office was in the capitol building, ran out to save the pieces. She documented each piece before sending them to the State Museum in New Orleans in the hope that they could be repaired. After reading about the effort, people who had collected "souvenirs" came forth to return the pieces.[23]

When talk about restoring the Old State Capitol became serious in the 1980s, the fence received its share of discussion, but that was about all it received. The need for restoration was recognized, but with funds so scarce, they were always allocated to work on the building. In 1984, a brunch was held to raise funds to save the fence.[24] A respectable amount was raised, although it barely made a dent in the then-estimated $500,000 price tag.

While the State House was being restored, the fence remained in a sad state. Chain-link fence filled the gaps where iron rails and posts were missing.[25] When the building reopened to the public in 1988, the fence was superficially repaired to appear presentable and painted green, but serious restoration was still a dream.

By 1996, the fence was in a disastrous state. Estimates for repair ballooned to over two million dollars. The escalating cost was a result of discovering lead-based paint on the fence. OSHA and EPA requirements placed the cost in the "high rent district." Steel straps were placed at strategic points to hold the fence together, stabilizing it and buying time until something more permanent could be done.[26] An ancient oak tree had grown to such size that it pushed a section of the eastern fence almost a foot out of place.

In the early 2000s, the legislature recognized the need for fence repairs and placed the budget request in the capital outlay bill, but as usual, state money did not stretch that far down the list of requests. Museum officials worked diligently to obtain grants and matching funds while keeping the project before the legislature. After hurricanes Katrina and Rita destroyed much of coastal Louisiana, it seemed unlikely the antebellum fence would receive state funds for restoration. But in 2006, the legislature once again included the project in the capital outlay bill. Those funds, augmented by some surplus exterior restoration funds, were used to contract with Robinson Iron of Alexander City, Alabama, to remove, repair, restore, and replace the fence. Repairs began in May of 2007 when the northwest quarter of the fence was removed, crated, and carefully shipped to Alabama. All portions of the fence have been repaired, restored, and replaced on a new foundation. Repairs were expected to take almost two years but were completed nine months early. Concrete has replaced the original brick foundation, and several protective layers of dark green paint now cover the elegant, historic, cast iron fence. The moss-draped oak under whose branches many governors were inaugurated was spared, but creative replacement of the fence was necessary.

Appendix II

Henry Watkins Allen Monument

Only one monument rests on the Old State Capitol grounds—the tomb of former Gov. Henry Watkins Allen, one of the most beloved men ever to serve the state of Louisiana. Oddly enough, Allen never served as governor in the State House. He was a legislator in the 1850s and took a personal interest in beautifying the State House grounds. During Allen's frequent travels, he sought out rare horticultural specimens to plant on the grounds.[1] Three ginkgo trees are among the exotic items believed to have been planted by Allen. One of the trees remains on the top terrace just feet from Allen's tomb.

When Louisiana seceded from the Union, Allen joined the Confederate army. He earned a reputation as a brilliant military commander who cared deeply about his state and his troops. He fought alongside his troops but was critically wounded and these injuries plagued him until his death.

In 1864, three years after the state seceded from the Union and two years after the capitol burned during occupation by Union troops, Allen was elected governor of the Confederate portion of Louisiana.[2] As governor, he earned respect by rebuilding the wartime economy of Louisiana west of the Mississippi River. He initiated commerce with Mexico, exchanging Louisiana products for the goods the state needed. Following the war, Allen, by then almost penniless, went into self-imposed exile in Mexico. In a letter to the people of Louisiana, he wrote: "I go into exile not as did the ancient Romans, to lead back foreign armies against my native land—but rather to avoid persecution, and the crown of martyrdom. I go to seek repose for my shattered limbs."[3] His supporters urged him to take his salary as well as a portion of the funds amassed by the state to help him reach Mexico. He refused, saying, "It is state property, and must be surrendered with the other assets of the State."[4] This selfless act was memorialized by an inscription on the south side of the monument, which reads, "Your friends are proud to know that Louisiana had a Governor, who with an opportunity of securing a million dollars in gold preferred being honest in a foreign land without one cent."[5] Allen himself chose the sentiment as his epitaph from a letter written to him by R. C. Cummings in 1865.[6]

In Mexico City, Allen became successful as a publisher of an English-language newspaper, but his health continued to deteriorate. He died in April of 1866 just a few days short of his forty-sixth birthday. His body, clad in his gray uniform,[7] was placed in a simple wooden coffin[8] and buried in Mexico. His friends were not content to let the beloved statesman's body remain in a foreign land and had him returned to New Orleans. When his body arrived in January of 1867, federal troops occupying the city refused to allow any ceremony, flags, parades, or other recognition of Allen as anything but an ordinary citizen.[9] A funeral service was held at Christ Church on Canal Street. A procession formed behind the hearse and was joined by thousands of people on foot as the casket passed through the city "without any of the forbidden accessories of music and military displays."[10] He was buried quietly in an unadorned plot donated by the city of New Orleans in a lovely area of Lafayette Cemetery No.1, near Prytania Street.[11] (Lafayette Cemetery No. 1 was at the corner of Prytania and Washington Streets and was often called the Washington Street Cemetery.[12]) Allen's remains were apparently moved several times. In 1885, the *Daily Picayune* reported that the body had been entombed in New Orleans four different times before a monument was erected.[13] It was not until 1870 that the Allen Monumental Association formed with the goal of erecting a suitable monument over Allen's grave.[14] More than two years later, in December of 1872, New Orleans newspapers reported that the monument commissioned by the Allen Monumental Association, made of Missouri granite and weighing five and a half tons, had been placed over Allen's grave. His chosen epitaph and other inscriptions had already been chiseled into the stone.[15]

After Reconstruction, a movement was born to honor Allen by having his remains interred on the newly rebuilt State House grounds. The legislature of 1884 appropriated one thousand dollars to transport Allen's remains and the monument from New Orleans to Baton Rouge and to erect the same on the State House grounds.[16] The site selected was on the north grounds about twenty-five feet from the edge of the uppermost terrace, halfway between the State House and the surrounding fence. The brick foundation and tomb, constructed in June 1885, were about five feet high.[17] The monument itself arrived in Baton Rouge by train on June 23 and was placed on the foundation the next day.[18] It rose about thirty feet above ground and was originally intended to hold a bust of Allen.[19] It is unclear if the bust was ever commissioned or placed on the monument while in New Orleans, but when it arrived in Baton Rouge, there was no bust. Instead a shapely finial adorned its top.

Governor McEnery invited the public to a Fourth of July celebration honoring Allen for "his military and civil services, his skill and daring in the field, and his eminent administrative ability . . . and providing for the wants of the families of absent soldiers, and in general to promoting the welfare of the impoverished and stricken people of his State."[20] The ceremony, described in detail by the *Daily Capitolian-Advocate*, was one of the most elaborate and solemn ever seen on the State House grounds. A stand decorated with evergreens and flowers was erected on the northeast corner, and a large portrait of Allen surrounded by a floral horseshoe hung over this stand. People eager for a good view crowded the State House windows and grounds. The tomb was elaborately decorated—a wreath of evergreen rested at each corner of the marble pedestal. The foundation and tomb were covered with earth and sod, forming a "quadrangular mound." The opening to receive the body was on the west side and was decorated with floral crosses, evergreens, and flowers. The north side was covered with magnolias picked from the grounds and a crescent and star from West Baton Rouge sat in the center. The south side was decorated with a floral cross, wreaths, flowers, and evergreens. The east side of the mound was carefully decorated with flowers spelling out Allen's name and was surrounded by a border of more flowers and evergreens.

Governor Allen's remains, by now placed in a new and more suitable casket,[21] arrived by train and were carried from the station up the rise of North Boulevard to the north gates of the State House. A lengthy procession formed and, to the cadence of military guns and the Silver Coronet Band, marched through town in a large square, beginning at Church Street (Fourth Street) and continuing along Main Street, Lafayette Street, and North Boulevard. The procession then entered the State House grounds, and Allen's remains were carried to the stand as young children tossed flowers on the path. The ceremony included prayers, speeches, and poems. Allen's sword was presented to Governor McEnery, who accepted and kissed it. Allen's remains were then placed in the vault and sealed. Following the internment, guests gathered at the garrison grounds for a supper with many toasts and tales of Allen's gallantry.[22] The governor, who had been denied pomp and ceremony when his body was returned to New Orleans from Mexico, had finally received the adulation the public wanted to give him.

Words inscribed on the marble monument are:

> (**north face**) Henry Watkins Allen, Brig. General in the Confederate Army and last Governor of Louisiana under the old regime. Born in Prince Edward Co., Virginia, 29th April 1820, died in City of Mexico, 22d April 1866. Hagan
>
> (**east face**) To the memory of Governor Allen this last memorial of love and respect is erected by an association of his friends.
>
> JNO M. Sandidge
> W. I. Hodgson
> Harry T. Hays
> ALF. H. Isaacson
> James Hagan, builder
>
> W. S. Pike
> W. C. Black
> Horace Carpenter
> committee
>
> J. S. Copes
> A. W. Roberts
> J. H. Wingfield
>
> (**south face**) Gov. Allen in letter from City of Mexico 25th Dec. 1865 to a friend in La—said When it shall please God to consign this

> mutilated body to its last resting place be it among strangers in Mexico or friends in La. I should desire no better epitaph inscribed on my tomb than the sentiment in the closing part of your letter.
>
> Your friends are proud to know that Louisiana had a Governor who with an opportunity of securing a million dollars in gold preferred being honest in a foreign land without one cent.
>
> Hagan

The west face of the monument remains without inscription. The *Daily Capitolian-Advocate* reported that in addition to the words already chiseled into the marble, the following statement would be inscribed on the west face of the monument:

> THIS MONUMENT Protecting the Honored remains of Henry Watkins Allen Is presented to the state of Louisiana for Perpetual Care in the Capitol Grounds, by the H. W. Allen Monumental Association, Baton Rouge, La., July 4, 1885. Accepted and Re-erected as per Act 47, Approved July 5, 1884, by Sam'l D McEnery, Governor.[23]

The words were never inscribed on the monument even though legislative act no. 47 stated: "That a suitable inscription of presentation by the Monumental Association to the State of Louisiana shall be cut into and on the side of the first block of the polished marble, as dictated by said Association."[24]

It is puzzling that the name James Hagan appears on three sides of the monument. The letters seem to have been chiseled as an afterthought. They are not the uniform, beveled letters of the main inscriptions, but are small and noticeably irregular. There is no evidence Hagan had any role in the return of H. W. Allen to Louisiana or in the burial ceremony. Senator Hagan was a member of the commission charged with rebuilding the State House from 1879 to 1882, but he was not named as a "builder."

Appendix III

Inaugurations of Governors Who Served in the State House

1. **Isaac Johnson, 1846-1850:** Isaac Johnson was governor during construction of the State House in Baton Rouge. He was inaugurated in New Orleans while the capital was still in that city. When the legislature met in Baton Rouge in 1850, he delivered an address before both houses gathered in their new chambers and expressed regret that construction was not yet complete.[1] Seven days later his term ended.

2. **Joseph Marshall Walker, 1850-1853:** Walker was the first governor inaugurated in Baton Rouge, but the ceremony was not at the State House. The Senate and House were engaged in "unimportant" business when they adjourned and met at the Methodist church. There, the oath of office was administered by Chief Justice Eustis.[2] Walker resigned after three years in office to comply with a provision in the new constitution that all offices be open for election.

3. **Paul Octave Hebert, 1853-1856:** Hebert was elected governor upon Walker's resignation. When the time came for his inauguration, he was ill with "brain fever"[3] and unable to leave his plantation near Bayou Goula. A committee from the legislature traveled to his home where they administered the oath of office.[4]

4. **Robert Charles Wickliffe, 1856-1860:** Wickliffe's inauguration was somewhat disorganized, as the planning committee had not much time to arrange an elaborate ceremony. Several groups arrived from New Orleans and met the Knights of Jericho, the Masons, two units of firemen, and a military escort on Church Street. Former governor Hebert and governor-elect Wickliffe joined them with a military escort, and they all paraded to the State House grounds. Once there, they discovered that "much to the surprise

of every one that body was found in joint session, hard at the labor of legislative business." Both Hebert and Wickliffe made a few remarks from the speaker's stand. Wickliffe must have cut a dashing figure, because ladies in the crowd commenting on his personal appearance disturbed the attending reporter for the *Weekly Morning Comet*. The procession then left the State House grounds for more festivities, culminating in an inaugural ball.[5] A few weeks later, the legislature appropriated $712 to defray the cost of the inauguration.[6] The article does not specifically state that Wickliffe's inauguration was held on the grounds, but a later article erroneously reported that every governor to date, presumably including this one, was inaugurated outdoors.[7]

5. **Thomas Overton Moore, 1860-1864:** Moore was inaugurated in the simplest of ceremonies. The legislature was in session when the Senate joined the House of Representatives in the House chamber to participate in the inauguration. Shortly after noon, Governor Wickliffe and Governor-elect Moore entered the House chamber accompanied by the "Chasseurs à Pied" and a band. Wickliffe delivered his farewell address to the assembled houses. Moore then took the oath of office and delivered his inaugural address.[8]

(Many governors served during Reconstruction following the Civil War. They were inaugurated in New Orleans, where they served their terms.)

6. **Samuel Douglas McEnery, 1881-1888:** McEnery was the first governor to be inaugurated in the restored State House after the capital returned to Baton Rouge. He served two terms but was inaugurated in New Orleans for his first term. In 1884, his second inauguration was held on the northeast corner of the grounds on a stand erected under the magnolias and live oaks. It was decorated with flowers and greenery, American flags draped artistically among them.[9]

7. **Francis Redding Tillou Nicholls, 1888-1892:** Nicholls was one of the few governors inaugurated on the south side of the

State House. The legislature convened in the Senate chamber for the administration of the oath of office to lieutenant governor. Dignitaries, accompanied by a band, then processed outdoors to a stand built against a backdrop of magnolias on the south side of the State House. The ceremony included the requisite prayers, music, speeches, and, of course, the oath of office. More festivities, including a pyrotechnic display and inaugural ball, continued in other locations.[10]

8. **Murphy James Foster, 1892-1900:** By the time of Foster's first inauguration, the ceremonies were becoming more elaborate. On inauguration day, many area fraternal and military organizations met the governor-elect at the governor's mansion and escorted him and other dignitaries west along North Boulevard to the State House grounds. A stand had been erected beneath the flowering magnolias and had been tastefully decorated by a committee of ladies. After the oath of office and Foster's inaugural address, cheers filled the air and cannons boomed in celebration as a military band performed appropriate music.[11]

Foster's second-term inauguration in 1896 followed a bitterly fought election, but by inauguration day, the mood was calm and happy. After administration of the oath of office to the lieutenant governor in the Senate chamber, dignitaries descended the spiral, iron staircase to meet Governor Foster. They walked to the stand built beneath the magnolia trees in full fragrant bloom. Foster and two previous governors, now Supreme Court justices, stepped up to the platform while Louisiana State University cadets presented arms and a band played. Following the music and prayers, the oath of office was administered and Governor Foster reverently kissed the Bible. There was tumultuous applause, and the band played "Dixie." Bouquets of flowers were presented to the governor, and after he retired to the governor's suite, well-wishers gathered for an informal reception.[12]

9. **William Wright Heard, 1900-1904:** Heard took the oath of office on a platform that seated former governors and other dignitaries. Prayers were offered, and the LSU cadet band played appropriate music. A huge crowd gathered on the elaborately

decorated grounds. Later, a pyrotechnic display dazzled the crowd. The *Daily Advocate* reported the fireworks were at the capitol, but clues from this and other inaugurations suggest it may have been at the university just before the inaugural ball.[13]

10. **Newton Crain Blanchard, 1904-1908:** Blanchard was one of the few governors to be inaugurated inside the State House. Plans were made for an outdoor inauguration and a stand was erected on the north grounds, but heavy rains forced the ceremony indoors. Blanchard took the oath of office in the House chamber beneath the speaker's stand. The huge room was packed with spectators. Hundreds of people could not get in the building and stood outside in the rain. Following the ceremony, a seventeen-gun salute was fired from the ship *Stranger,* anchored in the Mississippi River.[14]

11. **Jared Young Sanders, 1908-1912:** Sanders took the oath of office on a crowded pavilion erected in a corner under the magnolias on the State House grounds. The largest crowd yet gathered on the grounds to hear the young, dynamic governor. Following the oath, celebratory cannon blasts from ships on the Mississippi River alerted the city that a new era of politics was at hand.[15]

12. **Luther Egbert Hall, 1912-1916:** Hall was escorted to his inauguration by a large contingent of armed forces and dignitaries in parade. Upon reaching the State House, honored guests regrouped in the governor's suite before making their way to a platform built at the north entrance. Hall delivered his address before hundreds of onlookers. His inaugural festivities were scaled down as many parts of the state had fallen victim to recent devastating floods.[16]

13. **Ruffin Golson Pleasant, 1916-1920:** Pleasant was inaugurated on a platform in the shade of the oak trees. A crowd of ten thousand had gathered in Baton Rouge to witness the ceremony, which was described as "impressive in its simplicity." The oath of office was followed by a seventeen-gun salute and an inaugural address.[17]

14. **John Milliken Parker, 1920-1924:** Parker's inauguration brought trainloads of people from around the state into Baton Rouge. He greeted guests in the governor's offices at the State House before going to the university where the inaugural parade formed. Thousands of people marched in the grand parade, including

twenty-one brightly decorated cars of women urging ratification of the women's suffrage amendment. Once the entourage was on the stand erected on the north side of the State House, the inauguration was supposed to begin with a prayer, but the crowded stand settled a few inches, raising fears it would collapse. It did not, and the ceremony continued. The grounds were packed with spectators, and many were forced to peer through the bars of the iron fence to see the new governor. There was no cannon salute from the river as the *Dolphin* did not arrive in time. Bands played and Parker spoke, but the whole ceremony lasted a mere ten minutes.[18]

15. **Henry Luce (Luse) Fuqua, 1924-1926:** Fuqua was the first governor native to Baton Rouge. He was inaugurated, before a crowd estimated to be over twelve thousand, on a platform built on the north steps of the State House. Fuqua and his entourage entered the east door through a line of cadets before exiting the north door onto the platform. Tumultuous applause from the people of his hometown, as well as from around the state, greeted him when he arrived on the platform.[19]

16. **Oramel Hinckley Simpson, 1926-1928:** Simpson was lieutenant-governor under Fuqua but had the governorship thrust upon him when Governor Fuqua died in office. Simpson was in New Orleans at the time, so the oath of office was administered to him there by Supreme Court Chief Justice C. A. O'Neill.[20]

17. **Huey Pierce Long, 1928-1932:** Everything about Huey P. Long was larger than life, and his inauguration on the State House grounds was no exception. An impressive parade including military units, bands, and dignitaries formed at the university and wound through a bunting-draped town. Estimated to be a mile long, the parade ended at the State House, where Long was greeted by a crowd of more than ten thousand people. Those who could not get onto the grounds filled nearby streets and climbed the fence. Long took the oath of office on a stand erected on the north entrance steps. After the oath, cannons boomed amidst shouts of "Long live Huey" as gentlemen tossed their hats into the air. After the ceremony, Long entered the State House followed by hundreds of

well-wishers. Later that day, several band concerts were held on the grounds. An inaugural ball was held at the university.[21]

18. **Alvin Olin King, 1932:** In a calculated political move, King took the oath of office mere minutes after Huey Long took the oath as United States senator in Washington, D.C. The oath was administered by Miss Alice Grosjean, secretary of state, in the governor's mansion. The move was hotly contested by Lt. Gov. Paul Cyr. The mansion, State House, and other governmental offices were all occupied by armed guards in case Cyr made an attempt to occupy the offices.[22]

19. **Oscar Kelly Allen, 1932-1936:** Allen was elected just as the new state capitol was being finished. He was the first governor inaugurated there.

20. **Murphy James "Mike" Foster, Jr., 1996-2004:** Although Murphy "Mike" Foster served his two terms as governor in the new state capitol, he was inaugurated on the grounds of the Old State House in 1996. He chose that particular site for the ceremony because one hundred years earlier, his grandfather, Murphy James Foster, took the oath of office on the very same grounds. Foster, the grandson, patterned the ceremony after that of his grandfather's and even had some of the same prayers incorporated into the program. An elaborate stand was erected on the west side of the State House. In spite of a bitterly cold January day, spectators crowded the lower grounds and terraces to witness the event. Foster and his family gathered at the governor's mansion[23] and rode in limousines to the Old State House. There was a photo session in the building before the governor-elect and his entourage moved to the platform. Foster took the oath of office with his hand placed on the same family Bible used for his grandfather's inauguration. He then delivered an inaugural address of fewer than ten minutes. The ceremony ended with a military flyover and a nineteen-gun salute. A private reception was held upstairs. Foster and his wife Alice then exited the building to greet the crowd that pressed around him. History had, indeed, nearly repeated itself.

Appendix IV

The Merci Train (The Friendship Train)

In vivid contrast to the old Gothic State House, a modern railcar sits nearby on the northeast grounds. The boxcar was one of forty-nine sent to the United States by France following WWII. Noted radio personality and columnist Drew Pearson conceived a plan for Americans to help the people of war-torn France by donating and shipping useful items to the devastated country. The campaign was wildly successful and graciously welcomed by the French. After the war, they launched their own campaign to show their gratitude. French citizens from all walks of life gave what they could—a drawing, a plant, a doll—to say thank-you. Their generous gifts were divided among forty-nine boxcars, one for each of the forty-eight states and one to be shared between Washington, D.C. and Hawaii. The boxcars, designed to carry forty men or eight horses, were called Quarante Hommes et Huit Chevaux, or Forty and Eights. Built between 1872 and 1885, they were used to haul freight, but during WWI, they were called into action to transport troops. Following WWII, they were assigned to carry gifts of gratitude to the United States and arrived in New York aboard the *Magellan* in early 1949.[1]

The boxcar bound for Louisiana arrived in February with great fanfare. A parade of military units, university bands, and union organizations marched as dignitaries and pretty girls rode up Third Street to the new state capitol. B-52 bombers flew over the crowd. Gov. Earl Long (brother of Huey Long) officially accepted the boxcar from the steps of the new capitol.[2] The gifts were placed on display in the main hall, and for three weeks, crowds of people came to see them. Long named Miss Mary Evelyn Dickinson, director of the State Department of Commerce and Industry, chairman of a committee to oversee distribution of the gifts.[3]

The question then arose as to what to do with the boxcar itself. The grounds of the Old State Capitol seemed to be the perfect place for it. The former capitol had been dedicated to veterans of WWII in 1946, and the Old State Capitol Memorial Commission, composed of veterans and charged with administration of the building, was created in 1948. The boxcar was placed on the northeast grounds on a concrete foundation in April of 1949.[4]

On June 12, 1949, a formal dedication of the boxcar was the final event of the state convention of the Veterans of Foreign Wars. Drew Pearson himself was the featured speaker, and he broadcast his Sunday evening national radio program from the boxcar. A photograph from the *State Times* shows a large crowd, predominantly men dressed in long sleeves and hats despite the June heat, gathered around the train car. The housing—white columns supporting a roof over the car—was in place at that time.[5]

Louisiana has been recognized as one of the few states that adequately protected and maintained its boxcar from the "Train of Gratitude." Others have not fared so well; in fact, one was sold to a junkyard for forty-five dollars. In an interesting side-note, the boxcar to be shared between Washington, D.C. and Hawaii arrived first in the nation's capital, where it was emptied. The vacant car was then shipped to Hawaii with nothing but a bit of packing straw inside.[6]

Although Louisiana has protected and housed the boxcar, the gifts from the train are another story. They were distributed, but no one seems to know how or where, or even what they were. Newspaper articles from the time suggest a list of gifts found in the Louisiana boxcar and hint at their destinations, but the information has not been confirmed. (Gifts are mentioned only once even though they may have appeared in more than one article.)

From the *Times Picayune*, January 4, 1949, p. 7:

> a Sevres vase, a tricolor cord made from American and French flags flying from the top of the Eiffel tower when Paris was liberated, dolls (some 2' 10" tall)

Morning Advocate, February 23, 1949, p. 1:

boxcar with insignia of the cities of France which contributed toward filling it, numerous contemporary paintings, native trees, and shrubs

Morning Advocate Sunday Magazine, March 6, 1949, p. 11, (Margaret Dixon):

397 gifts for La.; Most gifts will go to museums throughout the state. French books including *French Without Toil*, French version of *Babar*, a 139 yr. old wedding dress, gifts made by school children, a cross of Lorraine made of francs, an ashtray made of mirrors, bronze statuettes, etched crystal wine glasses, paintings—one called the wine merchant of Alsace, dolls dressed in costumes of Brittany and Normandy, wooden shoes with sharply pointed toes, a small spinning wheel, fur-lined foot warmers, two bed warmers, doll bed and other doll furniture, a history of France, a portrait of Louis XIV, an imposing marble bust of Napoleon, swords, a piece of wood from Chateau Thierry, cord woven from flags, a huge drum from Marseilles, WWI relics, guns, and German helmets, a Sevres vase sent to Gov. (Earl) Long by the Pres. of France, two plates and several mugs all a century old, delicately embroidered linens, beautiful and fragile headdresses, numerous water colors, bronze vases, several handsome chests, two rubber balls, twenty bronze medals

State Times, December 31, 1953, p. 2, (Claude Moisy):

A French reporter found it very touching that the French and American flags were raised daily. Each of the 8 congressional districts received a part of the souvenirs. Some are now kept in museums or schools, in New Orleans, Shreveport, Monroe, Alexandria, etc. A few things with no special historical value were given to individuals.

Sunday Advocate, September 7, 1969, p. 7:

gifts were distributed to schools and museums throughout the state: 397 gifts, a 275 lb. bust of Napoleon, paintings, vases, books, pictures, dolls, jewelry, scarves, lace, shrubs, and trees

Notes

Chapter 1

1. The Isle of Orleans is the area bordered by the Gulf of Mexico to the east and south; by Lakes Pontchartrain, Maurepas, and Borgne to the north; and by the Mississippi River to the west.

2. *Baton Rouge Gazette,* 16 March 1850, p. 2.

3. *Acts: State of Louisiana 1825,* 86.

4. *Acts: State of Louisiana 1831,* Act No. 1, 4.

5. "State Legislature," *New Orleans Daily Picayune,* 1 April 1843, p. 2.

7. "What a Whopper," *Baton Rouge Gazette,* 29 May 1852, p. 2.

8. *Baton Rouge Democratic Advocate,* 28 May 1845, p. 2.

9. *Acts: State of Louisiana 1846,* Act No. 3, 4.

Chapter 2

1. An 1847 census showed a population of 2,523, which included whites, free people of color, and slaves.

2. *Baton Rouge Democratic Advocate,* 25 March 1845, p. 2.

3. Arthur Scully, Jr., *James Dakin, Architect* (Baton Rouge: Louisiana State University Press, 1973), 3, 86.

4. James H. Dakin Diary, Mss. #509, Louisiana and Lower Mississippi Valley Collections, LSU Libraries, Baton Rouge, La., 2-4.

5. LLMVC #509, 3.

6. *New Orleans Commercial Bulletin,* 17 April 1847, p. 2.

7. LLMVC #509, 14-15.

8. "Our Town and Parish," *Democratic Advocate,* 9 June 1847, p. 2.

9. "Notice," Democratic Advocate, 9 June 1847, p. 2.

10. *Democratic Advocate,* 7 July 1847, p. 2.

11. Act of Donation, Parish of East Baton Rouge to the State of Louisiana, 22 September 1847, Louisiana State Archives.

12. LLMVC #509, 52.

13. LLMVC #509, 39.

14. LLMVC #509, 53.

15. "Grand Celebration," *Democratic Advocate,* 10 November 1847, p. 2.

16. "Light Literature," *Weekly Comet,* 14 March 1855, p. 4.

17. LLMVC #09, 98, 100-101, 116, 118-19.

18. LLMVC #509, 77-78, 83.

19. LLMVC #509, 86-87.

20. LLMVC #509, 95.

21. Graham Lestourgeon, "Old State Capitol Opens Doors Again," *Baton Rouge Morning Advocate*, 13 January 1957, sec. F1.

22. "Great Fire in Baton Rouge," *Plaquemine (Louisiana) Southern Sentinel,* 5 December 1849, p. 2.

23. Bob Morgan, "Flames . . . over Baton Rouge," *Baton Rouge Sunday Advocate,* 5 July 1953, Magazine section 3.

Chapter 3

1. "Governor's Message," *Plaquemine (Louisiana) Southern Sentinel,* 30 January 1850, p. 1.

2. "Legislature," *Baton Rouge Gazette,* 16 February 1850, p. 1.

3. *Acts: State of Louisiana 1852,* Act No. 307, 208.

4. "DIED," *Baton Rouge Gazette,* 15 May 1852, p. 2.

5. *Baton Rouge Democratic Advocate,* 15 March 1848, p. 2.

6. "Removal of the Present Seat of Government to New Orleans," *Baton Rouge Gazette,* 10 February 1850, p. 2.

7. "The Seat of Government," *New Orleans Bee,* 4 December 1849, p. 1.

8. "La Nouvelle Capitale de l'Etat," *Le New Orleans Courrier de la Louisiane,* 3 December 1849, p. 2.

9. *Weekly Comet,* 30 October 1853, p. 2.

10. *Baton Rouge Gazette,* 16 March 1850, p. 2.

11. "Removal of the Seat of Government," *Southern Sentinel,* 20 February 1850, p. 2.

12. *Weekly Comet,* 19 February 1854, p. 2.

13. "The Capitol," *Baton Rouge Daily Comet,* 13 February 1853, p. 2.

14. "An Old Subject," *Daily Comet,* 12 March 1853, p. 2.

15. "A Very Excellent Suggestion," *Weekly Comet,* 19 February 1854, p. 1.

16. "Wonderous Condescension," *Weekly Comet,* 27 August 1854, p. 1.

17. "Removal of the Seat of Government," *Democratic Advocate,* 8 March 1855, p. 1.

18. "Another Order of the Day," *Baton Rouge Weekly Gazette and Comet,* 4 March 1860, p. 2.

19. *Weekly Comet,* 14 August 1853, p. 4.

20. *Weekly Comet,* 4 December 1853, p. 3.

21. "The Water," *Daily Comet,* 18 January 1854, p. 2.

22. "The State Capitol," *Weekly Comet,* 24 August 1856, p. 1.

23. "The State Capitol," *Weekly Comet,* 24 August 1856, p. 1.

24. "A Good Work," *Baton Rouge Weekly Morning Comet,* 7 December 1856, p. 3.

25. "The State House Grounds," *Weekly Comet,* 1 October 1854, p. 2.

26. *Weekly Morning Comet,* 7 December 1856, p. 3.
27. *Acts: State of Louisiana 1857,* Act No. 251, 246.
28. "The Gas Apparatus at the State House," *Weekly Gazette & Comet,* 20 November 1857, p. 2; and "Work on the State Capitol," 20 December 1857, p. 1.
29. "The Improvements at the Capitol," *Weekly Gazette & Comet,* 31 January 1858, p. 1.
30. "The Statue of Washington for the State Capitol," *Weekly Comet,* 23 October 1853, p. 3.
31. "The Father of His Country," *Weekly Comet,* 4 March 1855, p. 1.
32. "More Light in the State Capitol," *Weekly Gazette & Comet,* 14 November 1858, p. 1.
33. "Statue of Washington," *Weekly Gazette & Comet,* 2 January 1859, p. 1.
34. "That Temple," *Weekly Comet,* 23 September 1855, p. 1.
35. "The Close of the Academic Year," *Weekly Gazette & Comet,* 17 July 1859, p. 1.
36. "The Capitol on Fire," *Weekly Morning Comet,* 6 April 1856, p. 1.
37. *Baton Rouge Gazette,* 2 March 1850, p. 2.
38. "Music—Popular and Unpopular," *Weekly Comet,* 26 February 1854, p. 1.
39. "Anniversary Ball," *Weekly Comet,* 18 February 1855, p. 1, 3.
40. "Things About Town," *Baton Rouge Daily Advocate,* 31 January 1856, p. 2.
41. *Daily Advocate,* 11, 20, and 23 February 1858, p. 2.
42. *Daily Advocate,* 19 March 1858, p. 2.
43. "Arrived," *Daily Advocate,* 16 January 1857, p. 2.
44. *Acts: State of Louisiana 1854,* Act No. 22, 162.
45. "The State House Grounds," *Weekly Comet,* 1 October 1854, p. 2.
46. "The Capitol Grounds," *Weekly Comet,* 7 January 1855, p. 2.
47. "Work at the Capitol," *Weekly Gazette & Comet,* 31 January 1859, p. 2.
48. "The Grounds About the Capitol," *Weekly Gazette & Comet,* 31 July 1859, p. 1.
49. "The Close of the Academic Year," *Weekly Gazette & Comet,* 17 July 1859, p. 1.

Chapter 4

1. *Acts of Louisiana, Regular Session 1860,* Joint Resolution No. 199, 147.
2. "The Extraordinary Session," *Baton Rouge Gazette & Comet,* [Baton Rouge] 8 December 1860, p. 4.
3. "Now Then, What Next?," *Baton Rouge Weekly Gazette & Comet,* 2 February 1861, p. 1.

4. "Adelina Patti at the Capitol," *Weekly Gazette & Comet,* 30 January 1861, p. 2.

5. "A Word of Advice," *Capitolian-Advocate,* 11 February 1862, p. 2.

6. "Letters of General Thomas Williams, 1862," *American Historical Review* 14 (1909): 318-19.

7. "A Lifetime of Devotion: Baton Rouge Through the Eyes of Photographer Andrew D. Lytle, 1857-1917," edited by Merle R. Suhayda (Baton Rouge: Louisiana State University, 1999), compact disc.

8. J. F. Moors, *History of the 52nd Regiment, Massachusetts Volunteers,* (Boston: Press of G. H. Ellis, 1893), 33.

9. "The State House, Baton Rouge, Entirely Destroyed by Fire," *Weekly Gazette & Comet,* 31 December 1862, p. 2.

10. *War of the Rebellion: A Compilation of the Official Records of the Union and Confederate Armies,* U. S. Congress, prepared for War Department by Lt. Col. Robert N. Scott (Washington D.C.: Government Printing Office, 1886), ser. I, vol. XV: 630-33.

11. "The State House Grounds," *Weekly Gazette & Comet,* 26 March 1864, p. 2.

12. "All Around Town," *Baton Rouge Tri-Weekly Advocate,* 21 August 1865, p. 2.

13. "An Outrage," *Baton Rouge Weekly Advocate,* 30 November 1868, p. 3.

14. "The State Capitol," *Tri-Weekly Advocate,* 6 September 1865, p. 2.

15. "Louisiana Legislature," *Baton Rouge Tri-Weekly Gazette & Comet,* 21 December 1865, p. 2.

16. *New Orleans Bee,* 2 February 1866, p. 1.

17. *War of the Rebellion,* ser. I, vol. XV: 555

18. *Acts of Louisiana, Extra Session 1865,* Joint Resolution No. 3, 6.

19. *Tri-Weekly Advocate,* 29 March 1869, p. 2.

20. "Gov. H. W. Allen," *Weekly Gazette & Comet,* 11 February 1881, p. 4.

21. "Fire at the Fair Grounds," *New Orleans Times,* 6 March 1871, p. 1

Chapter 5

1. "To the People," *Baton Rouge Weekly Advocate,* 26 July 1878, p. 4.

2. "The State House Bill," *New Orleans Daily Picayune,* 2 March 1875, p. 2.

3. *Acts: State of Louisiana 1877,* Act No. 72, 110.

4. "To the People," *Weekly Advocate,* 26 July 1878, p. 4.

5. "What It Will Cost to Repair the State House, *Weekly Advocate,* 8 February 1878, p. 3.

6. "Un Peril Public," *L'Abeille de la Nouvelle Orleans,* 3 February 1878, p. 1.

7. "A Reply to the *New Orleans Bee*," *Weekly Advocate,* 8 February 1878, p. 1.

8. "The Celebration," *Weekly Advocate,* 5 July 1878, p. 4.

9. "Removal of the Capital," *Daily Picayune,* 9 November 1878, p. 4.

10. "The State Capital Vote," *Weekly Advocate,* 15 November 1878, p. 4.

11. "The Capital at Baton Rouge," *Baton Rouge Louisiana Capitolian,* 8 February 1879, p. 1.

12. "Why Baton Rouge Will Be the Capital," *Louisiana Capitolian,* 29 March 1879, p. 2.

13. "The State Capital!," *Louisiana Capitolian,* 10 May 1879, p. 2.

14. "The State Capital! Opinions of the Press," *Louisiana Capitolian,* 17 May 1879, p. 1.

15. "Baton Rouge Comes to Time!," *Louisiana Capitolian,* 24 April 1880, p. 2.

16. "We Are Too Modest," *Louisiana Capitolian,* 12 July 1879, p. 2.

Chapter 6

1. "The Victory is Won," *Baton Rouge Louisiana Capitolian,* 3 April 1880, p. 2.

2. "The State House at Baton Rouge," *New Orleans Daily Picayune,* 23 February 1880, p. 1.

3. *Acts: State of Louisiana 1880,* Act No. 65, 61.

4. "Proceedings of the State House Commission," *Louisiana Capitolian,* 27 May 1880, p. 3.

5. *Louisiana Capitolian,* 11 May 1880, p. 3.

6. J. W. Frankenbush, "William Freret" in *A Dictionary of Louisiana Biography, Vol. I,* ed. Glenn R. Conrad (New Orleans: Louisiana Historical Association, 1988), 325.

7. "Plans for the State House," *New Orleans Times,* 16 May 1880, p. 3.

8. "Proceedings of the State-House Commission, *Louisiana Capitolian,* 27 May 1880, p. 3.

9. "The Other Side," *Louisiana Capitolian,* 26 August 1880, p. 1.

10. "Baton Rouge Comes to Time," *Louisiana Capitolian,* 24 April 1880, p. 2.

11. "Those $35,000," *Louisiana Capitolian,* 22 June 1880, p. 3.

12. "Repudiation Again," *Baton Rouge Capitolian-Advocate,* 23 January 1882, p. 2.

13. "The New Capitol," *Louisiana Capitolian,* 6 July 1880, p. 3.

14. *Louisiana Capitolian,* 29 July 1880, p. 3.

15. "The Capitol," *Louisiana Capitolian,* 19 August 1880, p. 3.

16. "The State House Board," *Louisiana Capitolian,* 24 August 1880, p. 3.

17. "The Other Side," *Louisiana Capitolian,* 26 August 1880, p. 1.
18. *Louisiana Capitolian,* 19 October 1880, p. 3.
19. *Louisiana Capitolian,* 2 December 1880, p. 3.
20. "The Capitol," *Louisiana Capitolian,* 15 March 1881, p. 3.
21. "Progress of the Capitol," *Louisiana Capitolian,* 24 May 1881, p. 3.
22. "A Talk at the State House," *Baton Rouge Weekly Advocate,* 7 October 1881, p. 5, supplement.
23. "The State House Commission," *Weekly Advocate,* 11 November 1881, p. 2.
24. "Repudiation Again," *Capitolian-Advocate,* 23 January 1882, p. 2.
25. "Run In The Ground!" *Capitolian-Advocate,* 30 January 1881, p. 4.
26. "Rightor Set Right," *Capitolian-Advocate,* 31 January 1881, p. 2.
27. "Set on Foot in New Orleans," *Capitolian-Advocate,* 1 March 1882, p. 2.
28. "State House Warrants," *Capitolian-Advocate,* 2 February 1882, p. 2.
29. "The Governor's Good-By," *Daily Picayune,* 1 March 1882, p. 2.
30. "State House Commissioners," *Baton Rouge Daily Louisiana Capitolian,* 6 January 1882, p. 3.
31. "The Capitol," *Capitolian-Advocate,* 3 February 1882, p. 5.
32. "Buttermilk in Legislation," *Capitolian-Advocate,* 6 February 1882, p. 2.
33. "At the State-House," *Daily Picayune,* 24 February 1882, p. 2.
34. "Capitol Moving," *Daily Picayune,* 26 February 1882, p. 16.
35. "Resignation," *Daily Picayune,* 1 March 1882, p. 2.
36. "Farewell Ceremonies," *Baton Rouge Daily Capitolian-Advocate,* 4 March 1882, p. 4.
37. "An Enthusiastic Welcome," *Capitolian-Advocate,* 2 March 1881, p. 3.
38. "A Sad Accident," and "Well Done," *Capitolian-Advocate,* 2 March 1882, p. 3.
39. "A Worthy Thing," *Daily Capitolian-Advocate,* 15 August 1882, p. 3.
40. "Meeting of the State House Commission," *Weekly Capitolian-Advocate,* [Baton Rouge] 10 March 1882, p. 9.
41. "Meeting of the State-House Commission," *Daily Capitolian-Advocate,* 13 March 1882, p. 3.
42. *Capitolian-Advocate,* 17 April 1882, p. 3.
43. "The Capitol," *Capitolian-Advocate,* 18 April 1882, p. 2.
44. "Capitol Building and Grounds," *Daily Capitolian-Advocate,* 5 May 1882, p. 5.
45. "Official Journal of the Senate," *Daily Capitolian-Advocate,* 10 May 1882, p. 4.
46. "Legislators on A Run—From Friday 'till Monday," *Weekly Capitolian-Advocate,* 14 May 1882, p. 3.
47. "The Capitol," *Weekly Capitolian-Advocate,* 1 July 1882, p. 8.
48. *Weekly Capitolian-Advocate,* 8 July 1882, p. 8.

49. "Work on the State House," *Baton Rouge Weekly Truth,* 30 September 1882, p. 4.
50. Mark Twain, *Life on the Mississippi* (New York: Bantam Books, 1981), 195.
51. *Capitolian-Advocate,* 24 April 1882, p. 3.
52. *Weekly Capitolian-Advocate,* 11 November 1882, p. 5.
53. *Daily Capitolian-Advocate,* 25 April 1883, p. 3.
54. "State House Items," *Daily Capitolian-Advocate,* 15 September 1883, p. 3.
55. "State House Items," *Daily Capitolian-Advocate,* 11 October 1883, p. 3.
56. "State House Items," *Daily Capitolian-Advocate,* 19 April 1884, p. 3.
57. "State House Items," *Daily Capitolian-Advocate,* 11 January 1884, p. 3.
58. "The Inauguration," *Weekly Capitolian-Advocate,* 24 May 1884, p. 1.
59. *Daily Capitolian-Advocate,* 28 June 1884, p. 4.

Chapter 7

1. "Henry W. Allen," *Baton Rouge Daily Capiatolian-Advocate,* 6 July 1885, p. 1.
2. "Distinguished Visitor," *Daily Capitolian-Advocate,* 1 March 1900, p. 1.
3. "A State House Commission," *Baton Rouge Daily Advocate,* 27 May 1892, p. 2.
4. "State House Notes," *Daily Advocate,* 28 March 1893, p. 4.
5. "State House Notes," *Daily Advocate,* 30 March 1893, p. 4.
6. "Brought to Light," *Baton Rouge Weekly Advocate,* 1 April 1893, p. 5.
7. "Capitol Grounds," *Daily Advocate,* 23 July 1899, p. 1.
8. "The State House Fence," *Daily Advocate,* 7 May 1902, p. 1.
9. *Acts: State of Louisiana 1894,* Act No. 73, 87.
10. *Acts: State of Louisiana, 1896,* Act No. 47, 82.
11. "Acts Passed by the General Assembly," *Daily Advocate,* 23 August 1899, p. 1.
12. "Elevator at the Capitol," *Daily Advocate,* 6 January 1900, p. 1.
13. "State House News," *Daily Advocate,* 25 January 1903, p. 1.
14. "Repairs at the State House," *Weekly Advocate,* 6 December 1902, p. 1.
15. "Grand Excitation Baton Rouge," *L'Abéille de la Nouvelle-Orléans,* 14 May 1896, p. 1.
16. "Foster and Snyder," *Daily Advocate,* 19 May 1896, p. 2.
17. "The State Capital," *Daily Advocate,* 1 February 1902, p. 2.
18. "The Historic Old State Capitol Damaged by Fire," *New Orleans Daily Picayune,* 8 June 1906, p. 1.
19. "Extent of Damage Done by the Fire," *Daily Picayune,* 9 June 1906, p. 1.

20. *Acts of Louisiana 1906,* Act. No. 162, 307.

21. "Bills to Move the Capital," *Daily Picayune,* 9 June 1906, p. 1.

22. "Governor signs contract for Rebuilding the Senate Wing," *Baton Rouge Daily State,* 19 January 1907, p. 3.

23. "The Scrap Iron from Capitol Will Bring A Large Sum," *Daily State,* 4 March 1907, p. 9.

24. "New Lights for State House," *Daily State,* 16 July 1907, p. 1.

25. "Senate Now Fixed for Session," *Daily State,* 7 November 1907, p. 1.

26. "Furniture for Senate Chamber," *Daily State,* 6 February 1908, p. 7.

27. "Famous Painting Now Restored," *Daily State,* 15 May 1907, p. 3.

Chapter 8

1. "Capitol Elevator Stopped," *Baton Rouge Daily State,* 6 November 1906, p. 1.

2. "Elevating News for State House," *Baton Rouge State Times,* 13 September 1917, p. 4.

3. "Damage by Storm Will Amount to Thousands," *Baton Rouge Daily State-Times,* 31 May 1909, p. 1.

4. "Wires Go Under Ground Leading to the Capitol," *Daily State Times,* 27 April 1910, p. 1.

5. "Favorable Report Made on M'Clanahan Removal Bill," *State Times,* 28 May 1914, p. 1.

6. "Alexandria Swaps Votes in Its Fight on Baton Rouge," *State Times,* 29 May 1914, p. 15.

7. "House by Overwhelming Vote Decides Against Removal of Capitol to Alexandria," *State Times,* 9 June 1914, p. 1.

8. "One Grows Weary," *State Times,* 10 May 1920, p. 2.

9. James K. Keeling, "Louisiana State House Gem of Architectural Beauty," *New Orleans Times Picayune Magazine,* 11 June 1922, 3.

10. "Alexandria Renews Fight for Capital," *State Times,* 31 May 1922, p. 1.

11. "Wheat and Barley Grown upon State House Grounds," *State Times,* 5 October 1917, p. 4.

12. "Dance Thursday Night at State House Successful," *State Times,* 16 August 1918, p. 1.

13. "Grand Pageant at State House This Afternoon," *State Times,* 29 June 1920, p. 6.

14. "Amid Cheers House Returns to Use of Voting Machine," *State Times,* 30 June 1922, p. 2.

15. "Makin' the Rounds with Willie," *State Times,* 11 July 1922, p. 3.

16. "New $3,000,000 Capitol Building in Recommended," *State Times,* 17 May 1928, p. 1.

17. "Long Seems to Be in Control of Both Houses," *State Times,* 12 May 1928, p. 1.

18. "New Executive Takes Oath of Office and is Acclaimed by Cheers of Vast Crowds," *State Times,* 21 May 1928, p. 1.

19. "Ancient Ornamental Turrets on State House Are Being Removed," *Baton Rouge Morning Advocate,* 9 October 1928, p. 12.

20. John K. Fineran, *The Career of A Tinpot Napoleon, A Political Biography of Huey P. Long* (Baton Rouge: Claitor's Publishing, 1932), 25.

21. "Ghost of Fake Voting Trick Walks as House Moves to Oust Fournet," *Morning Advocate,* 11 May 1930, p. 1.

22. "Governor Displays Growing Weakness As Battle Warms," *State Times,* 21 March 1929, p. 1.

23. Fineran, 69.

24. "Night Watchman Who Put Out Two Capitol Fires in Week May Lose Job," *State Times,* 15 April 1929, p. 1.

25. "$5,000,000 Is Proposed for Capitol," *Morning Advocate,* 17 May 1930, p. 1.

26. "Long Plans Leading to More Taxes," *Morning Advocate,* 23 May 1930, p. 1.

27. "Committee Gives O.K. To Capitol," *Morning Advocate,* 29 May 1930, p. 1.

28. "Constitutional Convention Plan Now Resolved Into an Effort to Evade Two-Thirds Basic Law Rule," *State Times,* 13 June 1930, p. 1.

29. "Adjournment of House Is Beaten by Chief Lobbyist," *State Times,* 20 June 1930, p. 1.

30. "Long Forced to Give up Effort to Abandon Rule," *Morning Advocate,* 22 June 1930, p. 1.

31. Annette Duchein, "Louisiana's Historic Capitol Soon Will Pass into Discard," *Times Picayune,* 16 November 1930, p. 22.

32. "Ouster Against King Appears to Be Likely Soon," *State Times,* 27 January 1932, p. 1.

33. "Old Statehouse Sentiment," *State Times,* 14 May 1932, p. 6.

Chapter 9

1. James H. Gillis, "Rebuilding Work On Old Capitol Is Started by WPA," *New Orleans Times-Picayune,* 17 November 1937, p. 3.

2. Orene Muse, "Old State House Now Has Appearance of Ginger-Bread Castle," *Baton Rouge State-Times,* 25 March 1938, p. 21.

3. "Old State Capitol Catches Fire," *Baton Rouge State-Times,* 13 December 1937, p. 1.

4. Muse, *State Times,* 25 March 1938, p. 21.

5. "Work of Beautifying Grounds of Old State Capitol Is Proceeding," *Morning Advocate,* 14 August 1938, p. 5.

6. Muse, *State Times,* 25 March 1938, p. 21.

7. "Historic Landmark Undergoes Face-Lifting," *Morning Advocate,* 21 November 1937, sec. A2.

8. Muse, *State Times,* 25 March 1938, p. 21.

9. Roland T. Huson, "Tree Comes Down to Earth," *Morning Advocate,* 13 February 1938, p. 1.

10. Muse, *State Times,* 25 March 1938, p. 21.

11. "$55,000 WPA Funds Asked for Capitol," *State Times,* 29 April 1938, p. 17.

12. *Morning Advocate,* 14 August 1938, p. 5.

13. "Old Capitol Is Historic Structure," *Morning Advocate,* 10 August 1940, sec. 2, p. 26.

14. Baton Rouge Unit, Louisiana Writer's Project, "Old State Capitol, A Sketch," 1940, 8.

15. "Letters From The People," *State Times,* 15 October 1942, sec. B14.

16. "Letters From The People," *State Times,* 9 October 1942, sec. A6.

17. "Old Capitol Dedicated At Armistice Day Rites," *State Times,* 11 November 1947, p. 1.

18. "Old Capitol Being Tidied Up for Spring," *State Times,* 27 March 1947, sec. B6.

19. Beverly Busby, "Old State Capitol Is Still in Use," *Morning Advocate,* 11 April 1953, sec. C8.

20. "Report Reviews Commission's Work At Old Capitol, Improvement Ideas," *State Times,* 26 August 1950, p. 2.

21. "'Merci' Train Boxcar to Arrive Tuesday Morning; Parade Slated," *State Times,* 21 February 1949, sec. B8.

22. "French Box Car Installed On Old Capitol Grounds," *State Times,* 15 April 1949, sec. A11.

23. "'Merci' Boxcar Dedicated Here," *State Times,* 13 June 1949, p. 1.

24. "$10,881 Voted For Repairs to Former Capitol," *State Times,* 29 June 1949, p. 1.

25. *State Times,* 26 August 1950, p. 2.

26. "Landmark Removed," *State Times,* 26 April 1950, sec. A6.

27. "New Elevator Installed in Building Here," *State Times,* 14 May 1951, sec. A15.

28. Busby, 11 April 1953, sec. C8.

29. "Old State Capitol Faces Close Order," *State Times,* 19 June 1953, p. 1.

30. Ed Clinton, "Rehabilitation Need Is Very Apparent at Old State Capitol Building," *State Times,* 16 May 1955, p. 1.

31. "Will Ask Legislature for Funds To Restore Old State Capitol," *State Times,* 14 April 1955, sec. D11.

32. Busby, 11 April 1953, sec. C8.

33. "Open Bids on Old Capitol Rehabilitation," *State Times,* 7 February 1956, p. 1.

34. Ann Magee, "Old State Capitol Renovations Complete; Few Changes Are Made, *State Times,* 8 November 1956, sec. B9.

35. Graham Lestourgeon, "Old State Capitol Opens Doors Again," *Morning Advocate,* 13 January 1957, sec. F1.

Chapter 10

1. Terry English, "Front St. Road Widening Project Takes Part of Historic Old Capitol Grounds, *Baton Rouge State Times,* 12 July 1961, p. 1.

2. "Betsy Pounds BR," *State Times,* 10 September 1965, sec. A8.

3. "Old State Capitol, Other Repairs Asked," *State Times,* 10 November 1965, sec. C21.

4. "Okay $250,000 Renovation, Repair of Old State Capitol," *State Times,* 1 December 1965, p. 1.

5. F. E. Shepherd, "$28 Million Okayed for State Projects." *State Times,* 21 December 1965, p. 1.

6. Gwen Stewart, "Old State Capitol Slated For Return to Late 1800's," *State Times,* 30 Jan. 1968, 5.

7. Roland Huson III, "Restoration Work on Old State Capitol Now Nearing Completion," *State Times,* 13 September 1968, sec. A13.

8. "Action, Please!" *State Times,* 10 April 1974, p. 1.

9. Dick Wright, "Old State Capitol Here To Lose Mustard Color," *Baton Rouge Morning Advocate,* 11 April 1968, sec. B10.

10. "Old State Capitol Leaks During Rain." *Morning Advocate,* 11 July 1969, sec. C15.

11. "Old State Capitol's Fence Deteriorating," *State Times,* 8 June 1971, sec. C1.

12. "Mending Fence," *State Times,* 25 May 1972, sec. B1.

13. "Oleanders Scuttled," *State Times,* 19 July 1972, sec. B1.

14. Nora Norris, "Old State Capitol Here Named to National Register," *State Times,* 6 February 1973, sec. B1.

15. Don Buchanan, "Controversy Is Looming Over Fence at Old State Capitol," *State Times,* 26 July 1973.

16. John Morris, "Old Capitol Has Another Crack," *State Times,* 25 March 1975, sec. B1.

17. Elise Hardesty, "Local Landmark Now Becomes National Landmark," *Baton Rouge Sunday Advocate,* 21 March 1976, sec. D2.

18. Joan Samuel, "History," Old State Capitol Associates Files.

19. Samuel.

20. Anne Price, "Capitalites," *Sunday Advocate Magazine,* 2 March 1980, 30.

21. Anne Price, "Capitalites," *Sunday Advocate Magazine,* 9 March 1980, 38.

22. Anne Price, "Capitalites," *Sunday Advocate Magazine,* 21 September 1980, 30.

23. Samuel.

24. Anne Price, "Mired in political ooze," *Sunday Advocate Magazine,* 9 August 1981, 38.

25. Anne Price, "Restoring faith, heritage," *Sunday Advocate Magazine,* 22 November 1981, 26.

26. John Ferguson, "Restoration a Must for aging Capitol, *New Orleans Times Picayune,* 10 April 1982, p. 3.

27. Anne Price, "Landmark decision for a special landmark," *Sunday Advocate Magazine,* 22 August 1982, 32.

28. Anne Price, "Architectural detective looks for the bare bones and fabric of Louisiana's Old State Capitol," *Sunday Advocate Magazine,* 6 March 1983, 34.

29. Marsha Schuler, "Old Capitol should be folklife museum, planners say," *State Times,* 3 November 1983, sec. B4.

30. Samuel.

31. Anne Price, "State's meaningful resource," *Sunday Advocate Magazine,* 18 March 1984, p. 23.

32. Anne Price, "Louisiana's pastime—politics good theme for a museum," *Sunday Advocate Magazine,* 25 March 1984, p. 23.

33. "Old Capitol restoration groundbreaking held," *State Times,* 11 May 1985, sec. B2.

34. Robert Reilly, "Notes From The Curator," Old State Capitol Associates 4, no. 1 (July 1986): 4.

35. Armstrong.

36. Anne Price, "Why the old Capitol is closed," *Sunday Advocate Magazine,* 31 August 1986, 21.

37. Anne Price, "New museum head wants Old State Capitol open, *Sunday Advocate Magazine,* 14 February 1988, 9.

38. Bobby Lamb, "Old State Capitol to reopen for visitors on limited basis," *Morning Advocate,* 24 March 1988, sec. A17.

39. Anne Price, "The Old State Capitol is back," *Sunday Advocate Magazine,* 3 July 1988, p. 5.

40. Cheramie Sonnier, "Old-timer is treasure of facts on Old State Capitol," *State Times,* 27 November 1989, sec. B1.

41. Mark Lambert, "Jetson now wants Secretary of State to run Old State Capitol," *Morning Advocate,* 28 April 1990, p. 1.

42. Anne Price, "Cabildo might get Old State Capitol's $400,000," *Sunday Advocate Magazine,* 21 May 1989, 23.

43. Price, 3 July 1988, 5.

44. Mary Louise Prudhomme, director, Old State Capitol, personal interview, 15 March 2006.

45. Cheramie Sonnier, "Politics fuel turf war over Capitol," *State Times,* 8 May 1990, p. 1.

46. Bill McMahon, "Commission proposed to handle operations of Old State Capitol," *Morning Advocate,* 11 April 1990, sec. 2B.

47. McMahon, 11 April 1990, sec. 2B.

48. Price, "Local control of Old State Capitol sought," *Sunday Advocate Magazine,* 15 April 1990, 8.

49. Bill McMahon, "Bill removing control of Old Capitol from museum board heads for House," *State Times,* 12 May 1990, p. 4.

50. Bill McMahon and Marsha Shuler, "Legislature's Opening enlivens Old Capitol," *Morning Advocate,* 17 April 1990, p. 1.

51. Anne Price, "Old State Capitol knocks legislators off their feet," *Sunday Advocate Magazine,* 22 April 1990, 7.

52. Mark Lambert, "Jetson now wants Secretary of State to run Old State Capitol," *Morning Advocate,* 28 April 1990, p. 1.

53. Raymond Jetson and James Sefcik, "Who Should Run Old State Capitol?" *Sunday Advocate,* 29 April 1990, sec. 15B.

54. Editorials, "Local Landlord for Old State Capitol," *State Times,* 11 May 1990, sec. 8B.

55. Frank Main, "Battle over control of old La. Capitol intensifies with bill," *State Times,* 7 May 1990, p. 1.

56. McMahon, 12 May 1990.

57. Frank Main and Cheramie Sonnier , "Old State Capitol may fare better, bill's backers say," *State Times,* 23 May 1990, p. 1.

58. John LaPlante, "Senate turning over responsibility of Old State Capitol to McKeithen, *State Times,* 26 June 1990, p. 5.

59. Andy Crawford, "Re-enactment kicks off restoration," *Sunday Advocate,* 9 June 1991, sec. 1B.

60. Carol Anne Blitzer and Mary McGowan, "Mason's preside at closing," *Sunday Advocate,* 16 June 1991, sec. 3C.

61. Price, 19 December 1991, 10.

62. Robert M. Reilly, "Renovation—A progress Report," *Old State Capitol Associates,* May 1992, 6.

63. Price, 19 December 1991, 10.

64. Robert M. Reilly, May 1992, 6.

65. Anne Price, "Old State Capitol ready for facelift," *Sunday Advocate Magazine,* 19 December 1991, 10.

66. "Renovation Information," *Capitol Chronicle,* July 1993, 4.

67. Renovation Information," *Capitol Chronicle,* January 1994, 4.

68. Karen Martin, "Capitol Glitter," *Sunday Advocate,* 3 January 1993, sec. 1H.

69. "Renovation Information," *Capitol Chronicle,* October 1993, 4.

70. Carl Redman, "Renovated Old State Capitol," *Baton Rouge Advocate,* 29 April 1994, Fun section, p. 18.

71. "Renovation Information," *Capitol Chronicle,* October 1993, 4.

72. Anne Price, "Old State Capitol nears completion," *Sunday Advocate Magazine,* 24 October 1993, 6.

73. Melissa Moore, "'It looks almost like it used to look...'" *Sunday Advocate,* 1 May 1994, 1.

74. Scott Dyer, "Foster Vows Service," *Advocate,* 9 January 1996, p. 1.

75. Mark Ballard, "Old State Capitol to be restored," *Advocate,* 21 July 2004, p. 1.

76. "Study suggests unity in museum oversight," *Advocate,* 7 August 2005, sec. 1B.

77. "Old Statehouse Sentiment," *State Times,* 14 May 1932, p. 6.

Appendix I

1. Arthur Scully, Jr., *James Dakin, Architect: His Career in New York and the South* (Baton Rouge: Louisiana State University Press, 1973), 185.

2. "Letters from the People," *Baton Rouge State-Times,* 2 July 1938, p. 2.

3. *Baton Rouge Daily Advocate,* 25 October 1854, p. 2.

4. *Acts: State of Louisiana 1854,* Act No. 228, 62.

5. "Notice to Architects," *Baton Rouge Daily Comet,* 14 February 1854, p. 2.

6. "The State House Grounds," *Baton Rouge Weekly Comet,* 1 October 1854, p. 2.

7. "The Capitol Grounds," *Weekly Comet,* 7 January 1855, p. 2.

8. Annabelle Armstrong, "Old State Capitol's fence guest of honor at gala fundraiser," *Sunday Advocate,* 18 November 1984, sec. J1.

9. Beverly Busby, "Old State Capitol Is Still in Use," *Morning Advocate,* 11 April 1953.

10. "Capitol Grounds," *Baton Rouge Daily Advocate,* 23 July 1899, p. 1.

11. "The State House Fence," *Daily Advocate,* 7 May 1902, p. 1.

12. "A Landmark Lost," *Baton Rouge Times,* 7 August 1906, p. 1.

13. "Wires Go Under Ground Leading To The Capitol," *Baton Rouge Daily State-Times,* 27 April 1910, p. 1.

14. "Historic Landmark Undergoes Face-Lifting," *Baton Rouge Morning Advocate,* 21 November 1937, sec. A2.

15. "Grounds of Old Capitol Get Beauty Treatment," *Morning Advocate,* 14 August 1938, p. 5.

16. "Old State Capitol Will Have New Dress for Greeting Early Spring," *State-Times,* 12 January 1938, p. 5.

17. "Letters From the People," *State-Times,* 9 October 1942, sec. A6; 15 October, sec. B14; and 17 October, sec. A5.

18. Terry English, "Front St. Road Widening Project Takes Part of Historic Old Capitol Grounds," *State-Times,* 12 July 1961, p. 1.

19. "Old State Capitol's Fence Deteriorating," *State-Times,* 8 June 1971, sec. C1.

20. "Oleanders Scuttled," *State-Times,* 19 July 1972, sec. B1.

21. "Mending Fence," *State-Times,* 25 May 1972, sec. B1.

22. Don Buchanan, "Controversy Is Looming Over Fence at Old State Capitol, *State-Times,* 26 July 1973, sec. A12.

23. Anne Price, "Historic fence smashed by ancient magnolia," *Baton Rouge Sunday Advocate Magazine,* 17 October 1982, 38.

24. Annabelle Armstrong, "Old State Capitol to receive support," *Baton Rouge Sunday Advocate,* 6 March 1983, sec. J3J.

25. "Restorations," *State-Times,* 24 May 1985, sec. B2.

26. Anne Price, "Old State Capitol fence stabilized; permanent repair expensive, *Sunday Advocate Magazine,* 1 December 1996, p. 19.

Appendix II

1. Sarah A. Dorsey, *Recollections of Henry Watkins Allen* (New York: M. Doolady, 1866), 48.

2. Miriam G. Reeves, *The Governors of Louisiana Sixth Edition* (Gretna, LA: Pelican Publishing, Co., 2004), 68.

3. Dorsey, 299.

4. "Confederate Treasure," *Baton Rouge Capitolian-Advocate,* 23 January 1882, p. 2.

5. E. L. Scott, "Historical Notes on the Capital of Louisiana," *Baton Rouge Daily Advocate,* 12 April 1903, p. 2.

6. Dorsey, 336-37.

7. Dorsey, 365.

8. Dorsey, 373.

9. Vincent H. Cassidy and Amos E. Simpson, *Henry Watkins Allen of Louisiana* (Baton Rouge: Louisiana State University Press, 1964), 160.

10. "City Intelligence," *New Orleans Bee,* 28 January 1867, p. 1.

11. "The Remains of Ex-Gov. Allen," *New Orleans Daily Picayune,* 25 January 1867, p. 1.

12. "All Saints' Day," *Daily Picayune,* 2 November 1872, p. 1.

13. "Allen," *Daily Picayune,* 5 July 1885, p. 2.

14. "H. W. Allen Monumental Association," *New Orleans Weekly Picayune,* 5 March 1870, p. 8.

15. "The Allen Monument," *Daily Picayune,* 1 December 1872, p. 4.

16. *Acts: State of Louisiana 1884,* Act No. 73, 87.

17. *Baton Rouge Daily Capitolian-Advocate,* 18 June 1885, p. 3.
18. *Daily Capitolian-Advocate,* 24-25 June 1885, p. 3.
19. *Daily Capitolian-Advocate,* 6 July 1885, p. 1
20. "Remains and Monument of Governor Allen," *Daily Capitolian-Advocate,* 29 June 1885, p. 3.
21. "First Day—Senate Proceedings," *Daily Capitolian-Advocate,* 12 May 1886, p. 6.
22. "Henry W. Allen," *Daily Capitolian-Advocate,* 6 July 1885, p. 1.
23. *Daily Capitolian-Advocate,* 6 July 1885, p. 1.
24. *Acts: State of Louisiana 1884,* Act. No. 47, 57

Appendix III

1. "Governor's Message," *Plaquemine (Louisiana) Southern Sentinel,* 30 January 1850, p. 1.
2. "Louisiana Legislature," *Southern Sentinel,* 6 February 1850, p. 2.
3. "The Governor Elect," *Baton Rouge Daily Comet,* 14 January 1853, p. 2.
4. *Daily Comet,* 20-22 January 1850, p. 2.
5. *Baton Rouge Weekly Morning Comet,* 3 February 1856, p. 1.
6. *Acts: State of Louisiana 1856,* Act. No. 152, 125.
7. "Blanchard Inaugurated Governor of Louisiana," *New Orleans Daily Picayune,* 17 May 1904, p. 1.
8. "Louisiana Legislature," *New Orleans Bee,* 24 January 1860, p. 1.
9. "The Inauguration," *Baton Rouge Weekly Capitolian-Advocate,* 24 May 1884, p. 1.
10. "Inaugural Exercises," *Weekly Capitolian-Advocate,* 19 May 1888, p. 3.
11. "Inaugurated," *Baton Rouge Daily Advocate,* 17 May 1892, p. 6.
12. "Imposing," *Daily Advocate,* 19 May 1896, p. 2.
13. "Inaugural Ceremonies," *Daily Advocate,* 22 May 1900, p. 1.
14. "Blanchard Inaugurated Governor of Louisiana," *Daily Picayune,* 17 May 1904, p. 1.
15. "Sanders Takes Oath As Governor Of Louisiana," *Baton Rouge Daily State,* 18 May 1908, p. 1.
16. "Luther E. Hall Is Inaugurated Governor Of Louisiana In Presence Of Large Audience," *Baton Rouge New Advocate,* 18 May 1912, p. 1.
17. "Ruffin G. Pleasant Takes Oath Of Office As Governor Of Louisiana For Four Years," *State Times,* 9 May 1916, p. 1.
18. "John M. Parker Now Governor," *State Times,* 17 May 1920, p. 1.
19. "Fuqua Takes Oath As Governor," *State Times,* 19 May 1924, p. 1.
20. "Simpson Sworn as Governor By Justice O'Neill," *Baton Rouge Morning Advocate,* 12 October 1926, p. 1.
21. "New Executive Takes Oath Of Office And Is Acclaimed By Cheers Of Vast Crowds," *State Times,* 21 May 1928, p. 1.

22. "Huey P. Long Is Seated As U.S. Senator; Alvin O. King Takes Governor's Oath; Paul N. Cyr Threatens To Take Office," *State Times,* 25 January 1932, p. 1.

23. "Foster Vows Service," *Baton Rouge Advocate,* 9 January 1996, p. 1.

Appendix IV

1. Manuel A. Conley, "What Ever Happened To Those Forty And Eights?" *The Retired Officer,* January 1983, 34.

2. "Gov. Long Accepts French Gift In Colorful Ceremony at Capitol," *Baton Rouge Morning Advocate,* 23 February 1949, p. 1.

3. "Many Presents Included In Box Car Given State By the People of France," *Baton Rouge State Times,* 23 February 1949, p. 1.

4. "French Box Car Installed On Old Capitol Grounds," *State Times,* 5 April 1949, sec. A11.

5. "'Merci' Boxcar Dedicated Here," *State Times,* 13 June 1949, p. 1.

6. Conley, 38.

Bibliography

Cassidy, Vincent H. and Amos E. Simpson. *Henry Watkins Allen of Louisiana*. Baton Rouge: Louisiana State University Press, 1964.

Dakin, James H. *Diary*. Mss. 509, Louisiana and Lower Mississippi Valley Collections, LSU Libraries, Baton Rouge, LA.

Dorsey, Sarah A. *Recollections of Henry Watkins Allen*. New York: Doolady, 1886.

Fineran, John Kingston. *The Career of a Tinpot Napoleon—A Political Biography of Huey P. Long*. Baton Rouge: Claitor's Publishing, 1932.

Frankenbush, J. W. *A Dictionary of Louisiana Biography, Vol. 1*. New Orleans: Louisiana Historical Association, 1988.

Moors, J. F. *History of the 52nd Regiment, Massachusetts Volunteers*. Boston: Press of G. H. Ellis, 1893.

Reeves, Miriam G. *The Governors of Louisiana, Sixth Edition*. Gretna, LA: Pelican Publishing Co., 2004.

Scully, Arthur Jr. *James Dakin, Architect: His Career in New York and the South*. Baton Rouge: Louisiana State University Press, 1977.

Suhayda, Merle R., ed. *A Lifetime of Devotion: Baton Rouge Through the Eyes of Photographer Andrew D. Lytle, 1857-1917*. Baton Rouge: Louisiana State University Libraries, 1999. Compact disc.

Twain, Mark. *Life on the Mississippi*. New York: Bantam Books, 1981.

War of the Rebellion: A Compilation of the Official Records of the Union and Confederate Armies, Series I, Vol. XV. Washington, D.C.: Government Printing Office, 1886.

Index

A
Alexandria, 58
Allen, Henry Watkins, 29, 32, 49, 90, 99-103
Anderson, J. L., 63
Avery, Daniel, 14, 16

B
Baer, Mike, 84
Bagneris, Dennis, 85
Bahan, Larry, 71
Bares, Allen, 83
Beauregard, 53
Bird, Thompson J., 40
Black, W. C., 102
Blanchard, Newton, 55
Blount, A. C., 50
Bogalusa, 58
Bonaparte, Napoleon, 10, 113
Bragg, Colonel, 29
Brashear, Walter, 13-14
Broussard, Jay, 74
Bryan, William Jennings, 50
Buffington, T. J., 39
Butler, Benjamin, 33

C
Cabildo, 55, 83
Campbell, Jerry, 89
Carpenter, Horace, 102
Congo Square, 21
Cook, George, 13-14
Copes, J. S., 102
Cummings, R. C., 100
Cyr, Paul, 65, 110

D
Dakin, James Harrison, 13-19, 39-40, 42, 48, 59, 88-89, 93-94
Dameron, Mrs. Irving, 77-78
Dent, Fred, 71
Desmond, John, 79
Dickinson, Mary Evelyn, 111
Donaldsonville, 10
Duke, Sylvia, 83

E
E. Eean McNaughton & Associates, 79
Evans, Niles P., 71

F
Favrot, Judge, 58
Fineran, John K., 61
Foster, Murphy J., 50, 52-53, 89
Foster, Murphy J. "Mike", 89
Foundry, Hill, 97
Foundry, Pearce, 77, 96

Fournet, J. E., 62
Fremaux, L., 44
Freret, William Alfred, 40-41, 48, 87-88
Friendship Train, 71-72
Fuqua, Henry Luce (Luse), 109

G
Gay, Edward J., 44
ginkgo trees, 99
Grand Lodge of Louisiana, 16
Grosjean, Alice, 110
Grover, C., 31

H
Hagan, James, 39, 41-42, 102-3
Harry, Robert, 45
Hayes, Rutherford B., 35
Hays, Harry T., 102
Hebert, Paul Octave, 105
Hodgson, W. I., 102
Hubert, Father, 29

I
Isaacson, Alf. H., 102
Isenberg, Albert, 71
Ives, C. A., 70

J
Jefferson, Thomas, 10
Jetson, Raymond, 84-85
Johnson, Isaac, 19
Johnson, Jon, 86
Johnson, Mrs. Stuart, 81
Jones, Ann, 97

K
Kellogg, William Pitt, 33, 35
Kendrick, Brian, 83
King, Alvin O., 65
Knapp & Totten, 15, 17

L
Lami, Eugene, 55
Landrieu, Mitch, 90
Leake, George M., 76
LeCompte, Ruth, 77-78
Linfield, Rev. Mr., 29
Livingston, Robert, 10
Long, Earl K., 71-72
Long, Huey Pierce, 57, 61-65, 83, 89-90
Lytle, Andrew, 30

M
Macdonald, Robert, 80-81
Madden, Ragan D., 83
Martin, W. C., 69
McEnery, Samuel Douglas, 39, 42-43, 45-46, 48-49, 101-3
McHatton, 17
McHatton, Pratt & Co., 15
McHugh, Tom Ed, 84
McIlhenny, E. A., 69
McKeithen, Fox, 85, 88
McNaughton, Eean, 80
Mechanic's Institute, 21
Monroe, James, 10
Moore, Thomas Overton, 29

Morgan, Cecil, 62
Morgan, Thomas Gibbs, 15
Morrell, Arthur, 86
Munday, G. W., 39
Muse, Orene, 67, 69

N
Nicholls, Francis T., 53, 79
Niles P. Evans, 71

O
Old State Capitol Associates, 80-81, 83
Old State Capitol Memorial Commission, 71-74, 112
Ole Bull, 25
Opelousas, 31

P
Patti, Adelina, 25, 30
Pearce Foundry, 77
Pearson, Drew, 71-72, 111
Pharr, John N., 52
Pike, W. S., 102
Powers, Hiram, 24
Pratt, William, 17
Price, Anne, 79
Prudhomme, Mary Louise, 83

R
Reilly, Robert, 81
Richardson, F. L., 39, 42
Rightor, N. H., 43
Roberts, A. W., 102
Robertson, S. M., 39, 42
Robinson Iron, 98
Roemer, Buddy, 86
Rosenthal, Elise, 83

S
Samuel, Joan, 80
Samuel, Mrs. Howard, 78
Sandidge, JNO M., 102
Sayes, Clinton, 62
Scully, Arthur, Jr., 93
Sefcik, James, 82, 84-85
Shreveport, 31, 63
Simpson, Oramel H., 60
Spencer, Mason, 62
St. James Lodge, 16, 86
St. Louis Hotel, 35, 44, 46-47
Stine, Dennis, 83
Strakosch, Maurice, 25
Stuckey, 53

T
The Battle of New Orleans, 53, 55
Thompson, Sandra, 78
Touro, Judah, 21
Treen, David, 79
Tucker, Mrs. J. A., 77-78
Twain, Mark, 47, 54

V
Vasse, Lionel, 72

W
Warmoth, Henry Clay, 32-33
Washington, George, 23-24, 33

White, Maunsel, 13-14
Wickliffe, Robert Charles, 25, 106
Wilder, George W., Jr., 71
Wilkinson, Mrs. P. Chauvin, 77-78
Williams, Thomas, 30
Wiltz, Louis A., 39, 42
Wingfield, J. H., 102
Womack, Milton, 76
Works Progress Administration (WPA), 69-70, 73, 95